Elizabeth R. Hill

Incidents and Appalling Trials and Treatment of Elizabeth R. Hill

From the plotting citizen confederacies in Worcester County, Mass.

Elizabeth R. Hill

Incidents and Appalling Trials and Treatment of Elizabeth R. Hill
From the plotting citizen confederacies in Worcester County, Mass.

ISBN/EAN: 9783337328399

Printed in Europe, USA, Canada, Australia, Japan

Cover: Foto ©ninafisch / pixelio.de

More available books at **www.hansebooks.com**

INCIDENTS

AND

Appalling Trials and Treatment

OF

ELIZABETH R. HILL,

FROM

THE PLOTTING CITIZEN CONFEDERACIES

IN

WORCESTER COUNTY,

MASS.

NORTH BROOKFIELD, MASS., RAILROAD ORGANIZATION.

THE TOWN'S ILLEGAL ASSOCIATION—INCIDENTS OF SHARP PRACTICE BY THE DIRECTORS OF THE NORTH BROOKFIELD RAILROAD COMPANY IN ASSESSING LAND DAMAGE, SURVEYED AND SET OFF AS THE MOST FEASIBLE ROUTE FOR MEN DOING BUSINESS IN NORTH BROOKFIELD—THE DELAY OF THE COUNTY COMMISSIONERS IN COMPLYING WITH STATUTE REQUIREMENTS — THE IGNORING OF MRS. E. R. HILL, PETITIONER FOR DISINTERESTED APPRAISERS UPON SAID LAND SURVEYED BY SAID RAILROAD.

Mrs. Hill demanded in writing, three different times, to the President and Directors of said railroad organization, for qualified appraisers upon the estate of which she was legally seized, which said surveyed railroad route cut through from north-west to south-east, and the only satisfaction for her prayers was "we shall not comply with your request and shall not assess your damage until after all others,"&c. They evidently determined to locate and build said road in accordance with their own wishes, law or no law, and to suppress at all hazards whoever should dare to vindicate their rights in accordance with the Revised Statutes. And as their designs and purposes have been accomplished without much notoriety or explanation, and as settlement upon all land damage claimants has been effected, except said E. R. Hill, for whose land, and character, and all, their thirst must have satiety; their direful hate and plotting against her because of her knowledge of their illegal proceedings, demonstration of which will be given in this book which I am compelled to issue that I may have a chance for legal vindication that bribery may not suppress. Simms, the fugitive in Boston, was not more a fugitive than is said E. R. Hill to-day. Driven from her own quiet cottage by this ruthless throng, who have stopped the improvements being made upon her own real estate which is largely her's from her father in whose name it has been for more than three quarters of a century. Said real estate being located so near the village, hundreds that work in the "big shop" and out, have wished I was compelled to give it to them, or obliged to sell it, and said "if it can't be got by fair, it must by foul means from her," &c.

Said E. R. Hill, being at this notable era correspondent to the Springfield *Daily Union*, was therefore present at all of the public town meetings. I will here announce to the reader that I am not a woman suffragist, but am for woman's virtue, character and common sense, which will vindicate truth, justice and mercy—that will do all in the power of her might to suppress this false, glittering life, which is bringing so much ruin on our nation.

Alden Bacheller, T. C. Bates, and others, drew up and organized through a series of blunders, a railroad company, calling upon the town of North Brookfield, Mass., to take action upon the subject of building a railroad between North Brookfield and East Brookfield. On the 26th day of December 1874, a warrant was issued in the name of the Commonwealth of Massachusetts, notifying the inhabitants of the town of North Brookfield, qualified to vote in town affairs, to meet at the town hall on Saturday, the 2d day of January next, at 7 o'clock P. M., then and there to act on the following articles:

ARTICLE 2. To see if the town will vote to become an associate for the formation of a Railroad corporation, formed for the purpose of building a railroad from North Brookfield village to East Brookfield.

ARTICLE 3. To see what action the town will take in regard to voting to raise money to aid in building a railroad to East Brookfield and act thereon.

The town meeting was held under the above warrant January 2d, 1875, when Augustus Smith was voted moderator.

Motion by E. Hill, seconded by John Hill, to pass over article 2 ; expression of opinions, *pro* and *con*, as to whether the motion opened the whole subject of a railroad for discussion. Thus they argued sharp and fiery. F. Walker related his interview with the President of the B. & A. railroad by himself; A. Bacheller exhibited a draft of the B. A. & Ware River, and the proposed Worcester Co. Central, aiming upon the four miles between North and East Brookfield, advocating the immediate building of a railroad to East Brookfield; John Hill argued for grades; J. F. Hebard wanted this vote decided, that something might be done more to the point at issue ; it was voted not to pass over the article. Thus meal bags and sleepers were hurled by the tongue with savage ferocity, till it was a question in the minds of some, which of the two proprietors would first go out and hang himself. T. C. Bates, with his scathing thrusts at all opposers of building the railroad, one would suppose the great interpreter of railroad economy, using Judge P. Emory Aldrich's name as an assistant adviser—nothing more.

F. Walker's spirit becalming itself, he brought forward some resolutions preparatory to making survey of the most feasible route between East and North Brookfield and estimates of the cost of construction, with regard to the business interests of the town ; also that a committee be appointed authorized to correspond with any corporation or individual who may be interested in the enterprise or in any other railroad which may be directly connected with our undertaking.

T. M. Duncan denounced the idea of a railroad to stop at North Brookfield—he was for a through route ; John Gilman was also for a through route and was consequently driven from the stand. Dr. Tyler moved to adjourn this meeting until Wednesday evening next, at 7 o'clock, January 6th, 1875. At this meeting, on motion of Alden Bacheller that the town vote to become an associate, with others, for the purpose of building a railroad from North to East Brookfield, A. Bacheller, Bates, J. F. Hebard, John Hill, C. A. Adams and others, spoke in favor of the motion. F. Walker thought more definite, reliable information relative to the routes, grade, tonnage and business to be accommodated was necessary. Dr. Tyler advocated caution and due consideration before taking such an important step; he was against raising five per cent of the town valuation; as he termed it, we were getting a baby on our hands which had got to be brought up on the bottle, and wisely advised the raising of but three per cent on our valuation, for the statutes on the 1st day of February next would prohibit the town's involving itself beyond said three per cent. I think too much of my native place to have it sunk in debt by this Boston bloat and glassware drummer, and a few more here, on the eve of bankruptcy, to be huddled into office, to filch the town of its industries, for their own and a few others' emolument. That old shop has always had its foot upon my throat, and that Boston bloat has got the poll tax payers and weak minded cusses rabid, to yell and shout at every bark he makes. I tell you, citizens, vote to raise but three per cent. on our valuation. J. F. Hebard got right up and said he must have five per cent. for the baby, which was applauded as mirthfully cunning.

The vote was taken by ballot, yea and nay, using the check list. The result was carried. Motion by T. C. Bates that the town now appropriate the sum of five per cent. on its valuation as it shall be made by the town assessors, as subscription towards stock in building a railroad from North to East Brookfield. The vote was taken as above and the motion carried. Voted to adjourn till Tuesday evening, January 12th, 1875, at 7 o'clock P. M.

January 12th, 1875, at 7 o'clock P. M.: A live town meeting, and Alden Bacheller is addressing the house thus: " I suppose no business can be done because the directors have not yet been chosen; that the stockholders have concluded that to go on safely we must employ legal counsel." Chas. Adams, Jr., also advised legal counsel, saying that the selectmen had requested him to act as town's agent in the matter, and as he now understood the duties of the agent he thought he could consistently with his other duties and engagements do so; but if it should prove that much time and labor were to devolve upon the agent, he should be obliged to decline the appointment. G. C. Lincoln thought the town should be represented in the choice of directors. F. Walker said it could not then be known what amount of stock the town could subscribe for under its vote; it might now be competent for the town agent to subscribe for a small amount, or more than the amount held by stockholders. Voted to adjourn this meeting to Monday, February 1st, 1875, at 7 o'clock P. M.

NORTH BROOKFIED, January 17th, 1875.

There has been a meeting of the stockholders for the purpose of organizing a Railroad Association. They proceeded to choose a board of nine directors, as follows: Alden Bacheller, T. C. Bates, Bonum Nye, W. H. Montague, Freeman Walker, S. S. Edmunds, Liberty Stone, T. M. Duncan, John Hill. Bonum Nye, President; T.M. Duncan, Secretary.

The directors have invited the town to become an association. The selectmen have issued a warrant, calling on all citizens qualified to vote in town to meet at the Town Hall on Friday evening, January 22d, 1875, at 7 o'clock, to see if the town will subscribe for and hold shares in the capital stock of a North Brookfield Railroad. The railroad corporation to be formed under chap. 53 of the Acts of the year 1872, for the purpose of building a railroad from North to East Brookfield.

To see if the town will become an associate for the formation of a railroad company to be formed under chap. 53 of the Acts of the year 1872, for the purpose of building a railroad from North to East Brookfield.

Readers, pause! listen! That marvelous Bates and Bacheller, who have been conversant with court judges and railroad presidents, which is their rallying cry to bring every voter a victim to their desire, their one idea, that a railroad must be built or the town is ruined. And every railroad meeting heretofore held in the Town Hall has been packed to its utmost capacity with boys and unnaturalized citizens, as well as voters, who shouted and stamped uproariously for every argument in favor of the railroad, and hissed the opposers, they being in the minority, Bates having a marvelous vocabulary of magnetic power over the ignorant and stupid. The railroad pulse is beating in three-fourths of the audience; 120 to the minute in my opinion. Bates, laughingly, informs the selectmen that the evening town meetings had not been legal. "You must pull down that warrant for town meeting on the 22d inst., at 7 o'clock P. M., and issue one calling a town meeting on Friday the 29th day of January inst., at 10 o'clock A. M." The warrant was issued. For further enlightenment of the reader, I will here interpolate a copy of H. Knight, town clerk :

"All previous actions of the town in relation to a railroad from North Brookfield to East Brookfield having been regarded as invalid, or at least of doubtful legality, on account of the holding of the meetings in the evening, and perhaps for other reasons, a new warrant has been issued, a new action been taken, as will appear from the following record.
"H. KNIGHT, Town Clerk."

On the 29th of January the railroad town meeting was held, in accordance with warrant issued, and articles in said warrant were acted upon as follows :

Second article, now taken up, G. C. Lincoln said, in behalf of the selectmen, they understood the law to provide that the form of a vote shall or may be presented by them, and he, therefore, presented the following form of a vote : "Will the town subscribe for and hold shares to the amount of ninety thousand dollars ($90,000) in the capital stock of the North Brookfield Railroad Company, a railroad corporation to be formed under chap. 53 of the Acts of 1872, for the purpose of building a railroad from North Brookfield to East Brookfield ?"

Some of the arguments, *pro* and *con.*, upon the vote under consideration, are as follows : Freeman Walker argued that before the town commit itself to that article, we should first ascertain where the road was to be located ; what it will cost ; how to be paid for ? The cumbrous expense of building said railroad upon the town was clearly set forth by him.

If he was going to jump a ditch, he first wanted to know how far he had to jump, He therefore moved that we raise one per cent. on our valuation to investigate this subject before we enter into the expense. We must know the facts of the case, and should it prove favorable he should be for the railroad.

Dr. Tyler spoke to the same effect. Erastus Hill spoke upon the same ground, but gave further reasons for Bacheller and Bates' railroad. Bankruptcy was at their door, &c. Bates' followers showing the beneficial results which would accrue, and hurling venomous slurs upon Walker, Tyler and Hill (but, O reader, he was not put into the felon's cell). And as Charles Adams said in a subsequent meeting, being aggrieved at some remark of F. Walker, with tears in his eyes: " That his feelings were never wounded to such an extent in public before as when the above statement of Bates' slurs was uttered." Bacheller spoke with Bates, also giving the statistics of the three routes surveyed, the estimated cost of each varying from $80,000 to $100,000. Fifteen minutes after 12 o'clock, adjourned for one hour.

Met according to adjournment, when the motion of F. Walker, to raise one per cent. on our valuation to investigate, &c., was rejected. The question was called for, and ballot taken by check list. Carried, more than two-thirds voting in the affirmative.

The following form of a vote was then presented by the selectmen, under article 3d : " Will the town become an associate for the formation of the North Brookfield Railroad Company, a railroad corporation to be formed under chap. 53 of the Acts of 1872, for the purpose of building a railroad from North Brookfield to East Brookfield ; and shall the shares of the capital stock of said corporation to be taken by the town be subscribed to the Articles of Association of said company ?" The question was called for, and the ballot was taken by check list, counted and declared carried, more than two-thirds voting in the affirmative. Voted, on motion of F. Walker, that the town treasurer be authorized to borrow such sums of money as may be needed to pay the necessary expenses in obtaining the survey, and such other expenses as may arise. *Illegal*, sweeping vote that! Voted, on motion of T. C. Bates, that we choose a committee of three to act with our town treasurer in negotiating for the loan to the amount of the town's subscription, and report to the town at some future time. Voted that the committee be selected by a nominating committee of three appointed by the moderator. The moderator appointed T. C. Bates, L. P. DeLand, J. F. Hebard, nominating committee. The committee reported, and the town voted Hon. Chas. Adams, Jr., Bonum Nye, and S. S. Edmunds, committee on finance.

Voted, this meeting now adjourn until 1 o'clock P. M. of the day of the next annual March meeting.

APPOINTMENT OF THE RAILROAD AGENT.

"Whereas, the town of North Brookfield at a legal meeting duly called and held on the 29th day of January, 1875, to take action relative to subscribing to the capital stock of the North Brookfield Railroad Company, and becoming an associate in the same, voted to subscribe ninety thousand dollars to the capital stock of said company. Now therefore, we the selectmen of said town of North Brookfield do hereby appoint and authorize Charles Adams, Jr., in behalf of said town to execute its vote as aforesaid.

WARREN TYLER,
GEO. C. LINCOLN,
JOHN B. DEWING,
Selectmen of North Brookfield.

North Brookfield, Feb. 13th, 1875.

(Endorsed upon the back.)

NORTH BROOKFIELD, Feb. 15th, 1875.

In accordance with the within appointment I have this day for and in behalf of said town subscribed the articles of association for the formation of the North Brookfield Railroad Company, the sum of ninety thousand dollars of the capital stock of said company.

CHARLES ADAMS, JR.,
Agent of said town."

(A true copy.)

Attest HIRAM KNIGHT, Town Clerk.

That the readers may know we had some other meetings in the evening beside railroad meetings, I will say Mr. Crane of Boston addressed the citizens of North Brookfield, January 18th, upon the bill issued by the Directors of the Bay State Transportation League. Also January 27th, Rev. Mr. Murray, of Boston, delivered an address before the Library Association. Subject,—Poverty. Those who were privileged to hear said address could not fail to understand. He was not ignorant of the effect of poverty upon the mental and moral size of men, and how great the difficulty of developing the higher moral truths in the soul, while his whole mind and strength and time were required to meet physical demands. He said of the passages of Scripture that made him sad, one was this: " The foxes have holes, and the birds of the air have nests ; but the Son of man hath not where to lay his head." He portrayed graphically lines between real riches and false riches. A man may build a house, and have every element of beauty within, and yet he may have done very little : while another man may never have built a house except the house of character, &c. Should this little sketch book, written in a stranger's home, ever come before the gentlemen above referred to, they will readily bring before them the lady reporter at their right hand, at the time above mentioned. This lady was thrust into a felon's cell by some of the foremost of said audience because said lady will not bow down and worship them.

I also find, January 28th, 1875, a report of mine reading thus : North Brookfield Union Congregational Church, and its Sabbath School, which was founded in 1854, have adjourned *sine die*. I also find with me another event in this eventful month. J. E. Porter, Superintendent of Schools in North Brookfield, and Prudential Committee in District No. 1 ; and Daniel W. Knight, Prudential Committee in District No. 2, have resigned on account of the censure cast upon them by vote of the town on the High School controversy. Mrs. Hill being sick with rheumatism at the time of said meeting, must give hearsay report. The High School teacher, who was being denounced (being a native of Wales, a few miles beyond West Warren, Mass.), told me he could not conceive of such a garrulous meeting as he was eye and ear witness to. James Duncan, Erastus Hill and others, being officially set down, especially said Duncan, scathing ferocious talk—but, reader, it did not frighten Bothwell, to put him in the felon's cell. He was thirsting for Mrs. Hill to locate there. That meeting was a disgrace to the town for all time.

The 12th of this eventful month the selectmen appointed J. T. Gulliver a committee in District No. 1, and the Rev. Mr. Harlow in District No. 2, to fill vacancies above mentioned.

As some people become exalted in about the same way and suddenness as the popping of a kernel of corn, even so ariseth T. C. Bates. His sudden thrust upon notoriety in our midst was the renovating and remodeling the First Congregational Church which he undertook by giving bountifully of glass fixings, as he was at that time drummer for a crockery and glassware firm in some distant city. Said business being so lucrative, that said Bates received $2,000 income.

Report has it that during the siege of getting old citizens to give up their pews, and hereafter compelled to bid off a sitting or sittings, as their family might demand, from year to year, was hard mental digestion for some of the old orthodox worshippers. But Bates and some of the supers in the "big shop," who are rising like leaven (readers, that kind of leaven to the virtuous moral person is a poisonous miasma), they must oust those old men and rich old widows out of the broad isle, that their sudden growth may be in advance, unless these "old fogies" "shell out"—their sittings will be in the "shady side of the sanctuary," thus they argued. Hon. Chas. Adams, Jr., was against doing away with the old-fashioned choir, in which said Adams and family had been head leaders, Mr. Adams ever contributing largely for all needed improvements, but that swelling man Bates informed Hon. Chas. Adams in divers ways, as report has it, "The choir could get along without him, and his flute, too." That remark was bandied round from social table to fireside, by some as nice and sharp, and to the disgust and contempt of others.

The church, on October 15th, 1874, was rededicated. I was present. The house is in modern style, fresh tapestry, &c., looked as much better as one feels after an ablution, and new clothes on. And conspicuous upon the south side of the gallery was this swelling young man Bates, his figure somewhat in advance of the other sittings, his eyes rolling constantly, his whole figure speaking "All know I gave these chandeliers. I have caused this work to be done. Yes, this is the Babylon I've built up. I'm to be first man in this house. Now, they can't do no less than send me representative after all my great contributions, treading down every obstacle, making this fit for me in my marvelous expansion." Whenever my eye rested on him the great magnifier was, as above, radiating.

During the repairs of said church its congregation, on holyday, had been invited to join in worship with the Union Church in said town. Consequently said church was invited to join the First Church during the winter till the selling of sittings the coming April, sittings being free to all during the said time. As the Union Church had been suffering and wasting away for years, to me, as well as to many others, it was most apparently dead. When it was reported to me the Union Church had accepted the above invitation, but were not quite ready to "sell out," &c., I made this reply : " Died, October 15th, 1874, in North Brookfield, Mass., the Union Congregational Church, aged twenty years. The friends of the deceased desire it to lie in state a length of time. During its repose the choir will chant ' How short and fleeting are our days ! ' "

The "big shop" too being enlarged, gave position for more "supers." They, too, must have some more public notoriety, and offered to contribute largely if the Union Church will open its doors (said church being now most in the proprietorship of F. Walker, said gentleman being legally seized of the same through the nonpayment of taxes assessed on pews owned by non-church members). Walker foxedly cautioned all these aspiring applicants, thus causing them to pledge specified sums, or even more if needed ; on those conditions the church was resuscitated.

I said the Union Church was colonized in 1854, through fearful dissensions (the name attached to it was, the Church founded in a quarrel). Conspicuous and foremost was said F. Walker, ever ready for a rebuff to our most able and much revered Rev. Christopher Cushing, colleague with Dr. Thomas Snell. At this time, the prominent bolters from Drs. Snell and Cushing's church were the Walkers, Duncans and Skerry; out of church were the Hills, Bigelows and Gilberts. My husband, then Kittredge Hill, Jr., joined this stampede, to my great grief. I went with him, that the family might attend worship together, but, e'er two years passed, this church was too mean for *him* to enter. I had—August 5th, 1855—united with said Union Congregational Church community (with F. Walker at my left hand, in the broad aisle, together with a score of others,—I am now impressed Bothwell was of the number—he is now, certain), to walk with them in accordance with the articles of faith of the Union Congregational Church. This church became so obnoxious to my late husband, that he forbade me and our son attending worship there. I persisted, and that act, together with Spiritualism, which the dissensions above referred to had opened a space for some issue besides quarreling orthodox, one other cause—before these two last mentioned—separated me from my husband. George F. Hoar and General Charles Devens were my counsel. When Devens enlisted in the army, (now) Judge Dewey filled his vacancy. I was divorced first, from bed and board, in 1859.

In September of said year, I opened a private school in Grove School-house, North Brookfield, Massachusetts; was very successful, having previously been teacher in South Brookfield, and Spencer and North Brookfield in 1841 and 1842, before my marriage. As Mr. Hill still remains P. M., my friends advised me to seek employment in Worcester. Therefore, in May, 1860, I personally applied to Otis Putnam, of the firm of Barnard, Sumner & Co., Worcester, to work in their cloak and mantilla department. During their seasons of work I was there employed till the spring of 1862. I took the charge of the cloak and mantilla department in O. A. Smith's store, Lincoln House block, Worcester, where I remained till I was prostrated with rheumatic fever, and was under medical treatment of Doctor Nichols, Worcester, boarding at that time with Mr. Osgood Collister, singing teacher. When recovered enough to ride home to my father's, there I remained for a long time distressingly lame. During said time an opening more agreeable to my mind was forwarded to me, from Miss Mary Dutton, of the Dutton Seminary, New Haven, through the agency of Miss Catharine Beecher. There, too, I remained till sickness—diphtheria —which was prevalent in the seminary. My second term I was sick some two or more weeks, part of the time having medical aid two and three times per day. (This said March G. F. Hoar, obtained by divorce, $3,000 alimony. My father died February 29, 1864.) I returned to my late father's house, unable to wait on myself from the ravaging effects of diphtheria still with me. The coming summer Bonum Nye, Colonel Adams and Captain D. W. Lane were appointed appraisers for my deceased father's estate. It was my mother's wish to have the whole house, together with land surrounding it, set off to her, as she was then sixty-six years of age (was married to my father at the age of eighteen, in the year 1813; my father and grandfather Tyler, owning said farm for a number of years); previously to said marriage mother never knowing what it was to move, I alone of the children joining my mother in her desire. As I was the youngest, I was the last to appear before those legally appointed three men, " to tell what I had to say, &c;" and the following is exactly what I said to the legal three:

Mother desires to have the whole house set off to her, as rent would be coming in, giving her some spending money, and the land in front of the house, between cemetery and lane, together with that east of the house—give it to her;. and then I wish an equal share with the rest. Could I designate my choice, it would be the west end of the farm, close to my late home with K. Hill, said Hill's residence being in court under a bill in equity. Bonum Nye replied: The Hills will not let you have that place, and you don't want it. The town will blame us very much if we do not give you a home in this house." D. W. Lane interrupting and joining Nye in his assertion. Adams was silent. The other two stating, "Mr. Stoddard and wife had both requested that we give you the west half of the house," &c. Reader, I was then feeble, hardly able to walk. I said, I did want my house, and the control of the dead bodies of my four lost boys, and Mr. Hoar says I shall get it. And as for the town's blaming you, if you don't do so and so, it's none of their business. I think Mrs. Stoddard would be unwilling to be set off herself in this house, against mother's wish. I rose to leave the room. In going out I said: You give mother the whole house, and the land she has asked for; and my mother heard me say it. Reader, you will be surprised to read the following: Those men set me off in parts of the east half of the house, giving mother the west half, thus twisting me from garret to cellar, above, around, below my mother; also, giving me the land in front of the house—the worst portion that could have been set to me in the whole farm, and in open violation of my request.

My mother was angered almost to frenzy by that arbitrary, overreaching, tenacious, *bonum magnum* Nye decision. The consequences I will not here give, as my autobiography is soon to be issued. And I do, and ever have, considered B. M. Nye the direct accessory cause of my mother's untimely death, April 29th, 1866. In March, 1865, said Hill's house was decreed me by the court, I taking possession of the same the May following. The house having been rented since 1859, without any repairs, was in a most dilapidated and filthy condition, but I cleansed and scrubbed till winter, completely worn out. The last week in December Jacob Smith applied to me to take charge of the school in District No. 1, as he had tried two or three teachers during the past three weeks, all leaving the school, &c. On the 1st day of January, 1866, I commenced teaching in said school, with fifty scholars, from A, B, C, through Greenleaf's arithmetic. And a happier, better disciplined school could not be found —putting aside prejudice—being kept five weeks opened beyond the other school.

I remained there three terms, till a Henry Sampson was

committee—who will figure hereafter—said he should not hire Mrs. Hill. At that time twelve weeks was a term, and two terms a year. The spring of 1866 I had a private school of over seventy-five scholars. My summer term in District No. 1 was an especially happy, progressive school, every scholar just teeming with happiness and good will. As there had been many serious ruptures in said school many times for years, Minister Keene and the Examining Committee were antagonistical to the school at the time of my taking charge of the same, January 1st, 1866. Therefore the weal or woe of the school was depending upon my ability or interest in their welfare.

Readers, permit me to relate an incident which took place in connection with said school my second week there. I boarded at Col. Pliny Nye's. One evening, with some half dozen scholars around me, who had come in to be assisted in learning their lessons—and there was also present Col. Nye, Mrs. Ranger and other members of the family—came in Mr. Ebenezer Nye (and his feelings were a type of seven-eighths of the district), and the main topic with the family was the meanness of the school committee, as adding fuel to the rebellion. Says he: "Good Heavens, we should all been at Westboro if Mrs. Hill hadn't come here." I turned to him and said, "I guess not—why, Mr. Keene, when in school last week, praised up the school, and prayed fervently for parent, scholar and teacher," and when he took my hand on leaving he says: "Your school this afternoon has as prosperous a look as any in town." Said E. Nye "Didn't he think he had brought on this improved condition? Pray for scholar and parent—his prayers don't ascend as high as the smoke of a house."

In the course of the summer term we had an omnibus ride to Cold Brook Springs, Mass., thirty of the oldest scholars participating. Said omnibus was driven and owned by James Duncan. And, in the morning early, as we were to start at nine o'clock, J. D. called at my house, saying he came after me to take me to the school house that I might keep the devils in place, besides I propose to have my pay before I start. I replied, "Every arrangement preparatory to getting into your omnibus has been planned by me, also your service fee, &c., is collected and in the hands of the appointed secretary of said company, anticipating paying for said ride ere they had it. Furthermore, there has been made, by my scholars, three large beautiful banners with mottoes in large raised letters with puro green cuttings: first motto, ' Happy Band ;' second motto, District No. 1; third motto, ' We love each other.' "

Reader, the native instinct of the banner boys showed itself when passing where the school committee lived, or others who they felt had wronged them. Those banner mottoes would be turned toward them with rapidity. J. D. being very happy with the money, and clock work proceedings of the happy band, drove us round the different streets in the village, halting in noticeable places to show us off. After a splendid ride we reached the springs and tested the medical waters and had a grove dinner. When through, Fannie Ranger came forward, placing a beautiful crown upon my head with appropriate remarks, which took me with such surprise I bowed my head and wept. J. D. came forward and said : " Hallo! crowned! You should had it some other color beside green (it being green and gilt). Mrs. Hill is too black to wear green." My only reply was a fervent kiss given to each scholar. Winter and summer I was employed. My fall private school numbered over one hundred scholars. Hiram Knight, having prejudicious spite towards me,* tried, with his might, to prevent my having a private school, saying I advanced those in attendance beyond their classes, thus *deranging* the school, &c. In the spring a private school of thirty-five scholars at my residence. Said Knight preventing my having a public schoolroom, in the summer of 1867 I taught on Ragged Hill, West Brookfield, eighteen weeks, in the old district of grandfather Tyler. At the close of said school, after great praise given to me, in the school a unanimous vote of thanks was taken for my extra labor and painstaking. A memorable incident while in this school—the first part of the term— while boarding at Coleman Gilbert's : One fine morning on entering my schoolroom a strong fume of brimstone caused me to say, whoever has brimstone with them please leave the same outside of the door, the smell is oppressive to me. In my usual round to assist and direct my pupils, that their lessons might be learned understandingly, and being called to assist a Howe boy, who had been absent from school two or three days, I asked him the cause of his absence. Howe: "I have been sick." Noticing eruptive sores between his fingers, said I, "What is the matter with your hands?" Howe: "Erysipelas." Elizabeth Tyler (my second cousin) arose and with propelling force shouted "he'd got the itch, and grandmarm says we shall all *ketch* it; most every one has got brimstone sewed in their clothes." Reader, don't imagine I told her to sit down for she did that after giving the momentous alarm. I quietly rose from his side, went to my desk (facing my school—upon every brow was a woeful quizzing smirk), Master Howe if you have, I dismiss you from school until you are in a healthy condition to be here. Howe and his sisters and brothers began crying saying he has not the itch; it's because we are poor makes them lie so about us; it's erysipelas that ails him. I rung my bell. Then said, Charley Sampson, "You go home; tell your father (the committee) to bring Dr. Blodgett to this schoolroom the earliest moment possible that he may examine T. Howe, and thus be able to inform us what ails said boy. Charley sped off with the alacrity of a deer, and Howe took himself off next without being asked again.

Mr. Sampson soon brought up with said doctor, and espying said boy, at home, called, found said boy diseased with the old army itch (it having been brought into the school by said family two years previous, breaking up the school, from which the teacher did not recover for three months). They then came to the schoolroom, Dr. Blodgett examining every scholar's hand, mine included, for I had commenced scratching, much to the *amusement* of *said doctor*. The doctor telling two boys, who had been with said Howe, to go home and be cared for in haste.

As the above gentlemen were leaving, or standing upon the school step, the eldest daughter in school of said family took her books and started to leave, crying and muttering "It's just 'cause we are poor, he hain't got the itch." I stepped forward, placing my hand on her shoulder, saying: "Martha, don't feel so; the disgrace will be in exposing others to the disease." She snapped round and bit my hand like a dog. Reader, my hand swelled so badly, Mrs. Gilbert had to poultice, &c., the same. It was the unanimous voice of the district that my instant resolute move saved the spreading of that hideous disease, and the breaking up of the school, which was, I think, just the meaning of that vote passed. The coming fall my private school numbered forty-seven scholars.

In the winter I taught in No. 7, my old native school house, boarding with Chas. E. Jenks. During vacation I fitted scholars for High School. The following summer taught in father Hill's district, No. 5, boarding at home; James Duncan furnishing me with a team, driven by his children, to and fro, during the term, for which I paid $25. Private school in the fall.

Winter of 1868-69 I taught in Spencer, District No. 5, a school of advanced scholars; Mayhew's book-keeping, single and double entry, was thoroughly learned, Robinson's advanced arithmetic was mastered in its every mathematical principle; Warren's Physical Geography was memorized by a class of five. Two members of the above classes commenced teaching in the summer term, and proved themselves then and since efficient teachers.

I will here state, Spencer has the greatest scholastic ability of any town within the radius of 20 miles. Reader, is not this the evidence of her business prosperity? I will interpolate my teaching in Spencer the winter of 1841-2 (at that time schools were schools. This frivolous flummery, which for a few years past occupied four-fifths of school hours, had then no foothold.) Day's Algebra and Adams' Arithmetic, was taken up, memorized, and practically applied, with as much care and interest as the gewgaws of the day are attached to the feeble minded pupil. The spring and summer I gave private instructions by the hour, and also taught school at my own residence. In winter of 1869 and '70 taught again in Spencer, No. 5. Gave them private recitations, at my own residence, in book-keeping, algebra, analysis, ancient history, physiology and science of common things. Summer term engaged and examined for to teach in New Braintree, district No. 1. Owing to the distance of boarding house I gave the school up—remaining at home, and giving private recitations, afternoon and evening, during the summer and fall. I was engaged by Superintendent Robert Beecher to take charge of school in district No. 3 in the winter of 1870 and '71. Sabbath afternoon, previous to the next morning (Monday) for said school to commence, said Beecher called at my residence, saying he came down Saturday evening, about 8 o'clock, and there being no light in my house did not cross the street; and he was in something of a predicament, the issue of which would depend upon Mrs. Hill's magnanimous spirit. "A young lady from somewhere came in a coach Saturday evening, to take charge of School No. 3, to which you are assigned." And it came about in this way: I was ———— and said young lady desired to go out in the country to teach the rude country lasses. Beecher: "I will give you a school of ten weeks, so much per week." Lady: "It's a bargain, I'll be there." Beecher: "Supposing she was joking, as you know I must carry my part; thus I am involved." I bowed my head and wept. Beecher says: "Dry up those tears; good heavens, you will have chronic rheumatism, diphtheria, miasmal fever, and the Lord knows what more, down in that sunken hole. Now I will guarantee you will have private scholars enough, and make more money in the end—deducting doctor's bill, perhaps loss of life." Thus I was confronted with no escape but surrender. Private scholars were forthcoming—young men from "big shop"— to whom I gave lessons in grammar, letter writing, book-keeping, interest and percentage, &c.; James Duncan's son, Wendell in book-keeping, and daughter, Viana Bella, in other branches, on whom extra time and painstaking were bestowed.

A few brief outlines of events, from my marriage, March 22d, 1843, aged 16 years, 2 months, and 26 days. My husband was 29 years, 5 months, and 23 days. My father giving me a large wedding and extra furnishing for housekeeping. Not a cloud was in the sky that marriage day, and everything equally bright and prospective. Rev. Dr. Thomas Snell, minister of my native town. After the marriage ceremony, while partaking of the feast, Dr. Snell remarked to my husband upon his fortune in getting me for a wife, adding some were more capable of being married at the age of sixteen than others at thirty.

January 8th, 1844, I had a son born, weighing 3¼ pounds, all dressed. Dec. 27th, 1846, my twentieth birthday another son was born, and lived till Aug. 16th, 1847. As something was in my family making a skeleton not bearable for a spirited lady, in October following I stepped from my husband's door, saying I should not return till my house was rid of that skeleton. The following January the skeleton was pledged never to be thrust in my place, if I would return to my apparently mourning husband and child—which I did with as much alacrity and forgiveness toward my husband as a mother ever gave her child, Dr. Snell arranging and appointing the meeting at his residence; and after conciliation joined our hands, repeating the marriage vow, and closing in lengthened prayer, still holding our hands. We then took up our abode in the village, renting a tenement in James Duncan's house, till we were building the residence I now occupy, which was decreed me in my divorce from Mr. Hill, in 1864. I will here tell Dr. Snell's advice to me, after my separation from Mr. Hill, from bed and board with $150.00 alimony. "My afflicted child I have married you twice to Mr. Hill, and from what you say, and others, he has no legal right to you. I now sincerely charge you, never to attempt to live with him again. I know the careful instruction you have ever given your son, and in God's own time you will reap the reward. Let us pray," and we knelt, and his wife and Abbie, in lengthy prayer. On leaving his house, at the front door with my hand in his, he says, "God bless you, God be merciful unto you and keep you safe from harm. Amen."

In 1854, June 10th, another son was born, and died April 17th, 1857, of scarlet fever and canker rash; as beautiful and bright child as was ever born of woman. His constitution baffled that terrible disease nineteen days.

Nine of those days the sufferer could not make a loud noise, owing in part to the hard bunches in his throat. I administered to his every need; seventeen of those days my clothes were not off, to lie down in bed. My aged father would come up in the morning, and watch with me every move and change of the lovely grandson; mother coming when she could, and would often say, " it seems almost wicked for you to do so much, and hold that dying child here so long." His strong father was crushed in spirit at the loss of his idol boy. Our neighbors and friends did for us all in their power to stay the great destroyer. My eldest son, then thirteen years of age, was struck with the same disease three days previous, and Dr. F. said he must die, but our pet darling would recover. The attachment between the two brothers was the purest of earth. The agony of the lone brother, when that cold, silent darling's form was borne from the threshhold, never to return, was heartrending to all, and fresh flowers were every week placed upon his coffin in the silent tomb for five years. The funeral solemnities were conducted by Wm. H. Beecher, then candidate for settlement over the Union Congregational Church, from whence Rev. Dr. Waldo had been dismissed a few weeks previous. The very name of Beecher throwing a mantle over the great ordeal the Church had been called to pass through. I had been a teacher in Sabbath School for years, commencing under the ministry of Drs. Snell and Cushing, and continuing (after leaving my own home church for the sake of my husband) when the Union Church was established. When the Missionary Sewing Circle was established in this church, at its re-organization I was appointed secretary and treasurer of the same, which places I held for years, or till my absence from town caused me to resign the position. During my secretaryship I corresponded with Lewis Tappen and Jocelyn of New York, of the American Board of Missions. And many choice gems of poetry are daily in my mind, sent me by them at that time. Thus I became very intimate with Mr. Beecher's family—every member of whom I revered, and esteemed. Mrs. Beecher's every word and action seemed hallowed, and never did I witness a rude action or uncouth saying in that family while they remained in our midst. But their superiority brought envious censure; and dissatisfaction from the querulous spirit born with the church, caused Mr. Beecher and family, after a few years, to become members of the First Church, instead of pastor of Union Church. Mrs. Beecher died January 5th, 1870; the family leaving, except Robert, the April following.

Mr. Hill was appointed postmaster in November, 1856, and held the position until 1860. When his wife I took charge of the quarterly settlements in said office, and when making returns at Worcester, I always used language as if in repetition of Mr. Hill, fearing ever I should assume "the aspect of pants." December 19th, 1858, twin boys were born to us, as if to replace the two gone to join the angel band. The first born dying the 6th of March following, the other on the 25th. Mr. Hill would often speak as if frenzied—"Am I never to raise another child?" And he would seem almost to curse God and man, for no fathers ever loved their babies more than he.

At this time spiritualism came in like a flood in our midst, yet the door was opened wide for some isms "to kill," as they said, "the fighting orthodox." Mr. Hill joined them.

After my separation from Mr. Hill, Mrs. Beecher was my sole adviser on all private matters, keeping and giving as circumstances required. Dr. Lyman Beecher and his wife being at his son's, Wm. H. B., at this time of fiery ordeal Dr. Beecher, taking great interest in my case, would, whenever I was going to court or to seek for counsel, ere I started, say to all present in the room, "let us pray," and then he would invoke the divine blessing and guidance on my every move. When the court granted my divorce, they also gave me $3,000 alimony, which had to be drawn through bills in equity, Mr. Hill's brother contesting, &c. My last court and all claims liquidated in said Hill family March 22d, 1864, just twenty-one years from the day of my marriage. My father died February 29th, 1864. The reader may think this strange mingling, but the conclusions of this pamphlet will solve the enigma.

The winter term of 1871 and '2, I was engaged to teach in Oakham; was examined for the same. After examination I learned I had one mile to walk from my boarding house; assigned to school; that was quite a set back to my feelings; always having heard in my younger days "of people going out of this world into Oakham," and then add one mile, loomed up too much distance for me to foot—and having an application to teach the grammar school in Wales —and an able teacher was wishing for the Oakham position, which I most cheerfully gave over to his charge. Therefore I taught twelve weeks in Wales, boarding with my great uncle Dr. John Smith; and my home, while there with him, was among my happiest associations. The scenery of its hills and dales was biblically romantic to me.

March 28th, 1871, a writ of tort was served on me, to answer to whatever James Duncan might allege against me, a private attachment having been laid upon my property by him the 16th of January before. When Newton read that warrant, a voice seemed to speak to me "bring an action before midnight! attach every thing he owns at once!" It was then about ten o'clock, the anniversary day of the burial of my last born babe. I accordingly took the noon train for Worcester, went to Bacon & Aldrich for legal advice. They being out on some special business—waiting in greatest anxiety till about four o'clock, and their not returning—and knowing my order must be obeyed—G. F. Verry coming up stairs (ever before my opposing counsel), I asked his advice; his reply was "If you don't serve your warrant on Duncan before midnight, it cannot be entered next court." He accordingly filled out a warrant, and I returned home, giving it to Luther P. De Land, who served it on said Duncan, closing his livery, &c. Said James thereupon had to bestir himself and get out a replevin, Chas. Duncan being his bondsman. It agitated said James very much, and when brought before Squire Beecher with his bondsmen, he repeatedly asserted "It was not his doings, somebody else has brought this about." Squire Beecher says, "How does it happen this private attachment was laid upon Mrs. Hill's real estate by you January 16th?" "Oh, he had that done when he was getting his insurance. But he charged them not to do anything about it till they heard from him again, and they promised it should not be made known, &c." Chas. Duncan said "there was a mink in the wall somewhere." Duncan goes to Dr. Tyler to have it hushed up. F. Walker shows his talons by getting Emory Jenks to come to me to effect a settlement. Mr. Jenks came, and in due time informed Mr. Walker how he thought a settlement might be effected, &c. Mr. Walker pompously replied, "it must be stopped, each one paying his own costs—and on no other ground." It surprised Mr. C. E. Jenks, as he had a different conception of his application to him for to get adjudication of the same. During the preceding month Mrs. Duncan was heard to take my name in a libelous manner, therefore a warrant was issued for her to answer to said libel—Mr. T. M. Duncan being her bondsman. Duncan was often heard to say "I'll not stop till I make Miss Hill spend her last dollar—I'll fix her." James Duncan being a man of questionable morality —Mrs. Hill having offended his fiendish purposes—refusing to ride with him, and telling his wife the reason why, &c. His wife and their son Charles coming repeatedly to my residence to heal and reconcile the breach of friendship so ruthlessly sundered by Mr. Duncan's known trait of character. Mr. Duncan coming with his wife at last, was ready to do anything, and ask my forgiveness upon his knees (the date of which I have in my memorandum at home), if I would only forgive and appear cordial in his family as before. I forgave—never to any one did I repeat his insult, except to Mrs. Beecher and Mrs. D. W. Lane—well knowing that with those Christian women it would be kept silent as the grave. Mrs. Beecher regretted I had ever repeated it to Mrs. Duncan, as she was known to be a jealous spirited frivolous woman; she feared her vengeance would be turned on me with the same vigor as upon some others in our midst.

Mrs. Duncan had often repeated, "if one place in town was cleaned out, the great source of her misery and jealousy, she should be perfectly happy," &c. And would add, "if that house ain't emptied of its inmates——will clear that nest out clean." And, reader, that nest was cleaned out in the dead of night during one of the most tempestuous storms known in our regions. When the insurance companies viewed the ruins, and learning the jealousy existing on the part of the family towards its inmates, he could not get his insurance blanket unless he could give some reason that it had been the work of an incendiary out of his family. I will here instance, J. Duncan had had buildings burned three or four times before this one, the "Old Tavern" being one. I was, at this time, in New Haven, at Dutton Seminary, and it was written me there, that the firemen's hose was cut repeatedly to prevent, as it were, the extinguishing of the flames. Readers, you will see insurance companies had been well bled by J. D. A tenant in said tavern, report has had it, was tenant in house last burned. And as I knew from his and his wife's own tongue the direful jealousy on her part towards some inmates of the house, and Duncan well knowing my word "would drop as the rain and distil like the dew," and that latent unsatiated repulse above mentioned, and to cover their own sins my name was thus ignominiously dragged into the Superior Court at Worcester. Duncan taking as witnesses, scores of the questionable minded, making gratuitous and bountiful spread of money, holding hundreds of dollars in his hands in bills, to be seen by all, tendering to those he had bought down there as mere tools. After a siege of five days—about three of which were spent in hearing Duncan's witnesses, each one repeating the same thing—"they heard so and so," not one of the whole number could tell for his or her life who said it. Duncan alone criminating, for which State prison for life ought to be the sentence, and would be, if justice were executed. Duncan and wife and Jane Dale having a written programme which they had made up with their own vocabulary—learning to repeat it from day to day, each reciting to the other, from time to time, Duncan often saying to them, "you got this learnt, you won't have the papers to look on in court." An eye and ear witness of the above told the same to Dr. Tyler, and that paper or its copy was used in court by their lawyer, thus attempting to criminate me, who was as innocent of the crime they were trying to allege to me as the blood of Christ. And I have yet first to believe that in no county, except the one mentioned, would such evidence be allowable on the court stand—neither in that county would such a scene take place before the war. As the sheriff and official places are filled with men whose only qualification was their love for sporting, especially hunting, having been trained in the army to hunt and kill. Literary qualifications were not an element in their being ; they learnt the requirements of their offices by practice, and if officers thus employed violate the law constantly —the defendants are too often in the place of the " Old Legree slaves," " d——n ye, we got ye, help yourself if you can," thus compelled to surrender. And if there chances to be one who walks in uprightness and truth, and scorns, and bids defiance to their illegal traffic, they are set upon as if by bloodhounds to save the spoils to the trespasser. And the advocate of justice and right is led to cry in anguish of soul, "Oh Lord, how long, how long!" The above court ended in my behalf, giving me a small pittance for libel damage! James Duncan not trying his tort and private attachment on my property case against me. As my case against J. Duncan was to be tried in April, I wrote my counsel not to fail to have the case tried, as I was ready to meet it at its every issue. Not hearing from him, I went down the first day of court, in said April, and reaching the court house before 11 o'clock A. M., my lawyer and his had just had it dropped. My consternation was unbounded, when the clerk of the courts thus informed me. I then betook myself to Duncan's counsel, to get his version. He said, he "thought it outrageous for me to be kept in court, when my time and services ought to be in the school room." He regretted the past proceedings very much, and the citizens of North Brookfield were not willing the case should be continued longer. I replied, they were willing James Duncan should use my name liberally to get his insurance, and save money to that quarrelling church, to which the Duncans were great contributors. Skerry and F. Walker (James Duncan not a churchman), without one iota of reason, except the money for their church, did work with might, to ruin my character. My case was being reinstated in court against J. Duncan, by counsel employed in Western Massachusetts; and as I was going to the post office in North Brookfield, with a letter to said counsel, on the 25th of said April, in passing the "big shop," where ball-playing in the street front of said shop, was and had been for years at times a dangerous nuisance—Mrs. De Devoise, only the Friday evening before said day, had turned homeward, fearing she would be killed in passing the playing crowd in the street and on the common front of Church,—about two o'clock said 25th April, by said crowd, I was struck by their club (wielded by Austin Adams), in this rabble, the blow falling just above the right temple. After I came to my senses, so as to hear, not feeling any pain, and in total darkness for a length of time, my vision returned, but dim. My brother dressing the wound, carrying me home, in which state of numbness I remained some two days, when concussion set in, and my life hung quivering for days. I endured excruciating pain for weeks, and not once during said sickness was my mind broken, but calm, ever sinking, when weary for months, I was unable to work or read. It was more than six months before I could stoop without nausea.

The following September, seven of the citizens called a town meeting, for the purpose of raising money as remuneration for injury received by me in the public street, by an acknowledged public nuisance. During time of said warrant (report had it), F. Walker, S. Skerry, bestirred themselves to bring out the class of votes who had figured at the court for said gentlemen, telling said men "there was no law holding the town responsible for said injury, and we must all be there, for there is a " set here " who are going to vote to pay her damages." "Don't fail to be there, we'll close that town meeting as quick as it begins." And, reader, they did. Nat. Foster, meeting me subsequently (my countenance being most deathly), said he, " How are you getting over your injury?" "I'm not able to work yet, sir, nor read, the utmost care I have to take of myself. It seems hard that top of that Duncan outrage I should have added to my cup this physical suffering, with loss of time, money, &c. And the town meeting held typifies the Christianity of this place. "You *needn't* think, or expect the town will pay one cent that it's not obliged to." I replied, "I'll make a minute of your statement, I am impressed, sir, that it will be brought to notice some future time; good-day." And, reader, but three church members of the church in which I am member, so much as gave me the cup of "cold water" during the above sickness. The very church that I had labored for, and contributed of my hard labor for its support years previous in open violation of my late husband's wish.

The inhuman treatment from said church, and in open violation of all orthodox creeds, caused me to withdraw from attending church on Sabbath day, till said church should comply with congregational usages, "when a brother is offended, &c.," not one word said to me by said body till May 16th, 1873, James Miller, Clerk Union Congregational Church, before mentioned, wrote me calling my attention to that part of the covenant which reads, "You engage to walk with the church in Christian fellowship and charity, to attend upon its ordinances, &c." Reader, even the minister of the said church did not call on me during my long sickness, notwithstanding I asked him to, at times when meeting him from home. Rev. De Bevoise and wife did watch with me, as their children had been under my instructions more or less since their citizenship; "baby" De Bevoise, Cora and Charley Sampson, James Roice, were ministering angels on earth at that time to their old teacher. But the church, oh where, oh shame! I think of you thus, "you will need Lazarus to dip the tip of his finger in water to cool your parched tongue in that hour." Should an orthodox minister chance to read this book, I trust you will hold the Union Congregational Church, North Brookfield, Mass., amenable to your discipline for this breach of orthodox creed, &c.

ELMIRA CITY.—At the close of the institute at Elmira, I joined the excursion to Watkins Glen, with hundreds of professors and teachers, among them one who was our instructor, and made plain the cause of this wonderful gorge in nature; in passing under one of the high cascades, where evident drenching, at the least misstep was inevitable, President McCosh and myself passed under, when the shout arose, "You will be Baptists when you get to the other side." Just emerging, sprinkled, said I, "Gentlemen shall we retain the name Baptist?" At 7 o'clock P. M., a party started on an excursion to Niagara Falls; I was very weary, but determined on seeing the falls e'er I returned to my home. Among the excursionists to the falls were President Northrup, President Harris of the National Institute, Abbot, Superintendent of Schools, Brooklyn; on reaching Buffalo, 12 M., I left said company to go to West Hamburg, to visit at John Smith's, eldest son of the John Smith before mentioned. As I had the day previous sent him a postal card informing him of my coming and asking him to meet me at Buffalo, upon stepping out of the cars upon the platform, within ten feet of me stood said Smith, and then waiting for the next train to take me to his pleasant home, glad indeed to remove my cindered apparel and cleanse myself of the blackening coal dust—which said vicinity has more than its double portion. His wife had a nice chicken breakfast waiting our coming, of which I partook very sparingly, saying, "you will please excuse me from every thing of whatever name or nature, *but sleep*, that great restorer, twin sister to death, and when I emerge from that I'll visit, to your heart's satiety. Thus, good morning," and I went to my room for said repose, pledging them not to call me, but let me appear, when fit thus to do.

The day was near its close before I could really force to dress, which was arrested on throwing open the blind; the broad front view, not thirty rods from my room lay a part of Lake Erie. Readers, there were more than forty, would not count the schooners, steamboats, sailboats, and whatever plies said lake in my broad view, each hurrying to and fro, with the rapidity of a dove, and as noiselessly, to me. (*That's a schooner!* Oh, William, your noble, manly figure, with mind so thoroughly versed in learning, ready, and in the vineyard inparting of the abundance thereof.) Just for a rest, with uncle's schooner, with pleasure sail, on the lake for Toledo, when, oh!! that treacherous sand bank stops the schooner. William and uncle swim for the shore. It's too much for William, and e'er eight and forty hours are numbered, the word goes forth, the remains of William Tyler will be forwarded to Capt. Roderick Williston, Sandusky City, Ohio, in next sailboat. William, that's not the schooner and sailboat I see,—I know!!!)

Cousin and wife coming along under the window, saying, "We hear you." "I am glad to have something that will make you seem natural (talking to myself); wife, and I have been saying we should not suppose anything but death could have changed you so, and all from that accursed set of ball players." In the space of forty-eight hours more we are standing at Niagara Falls, on Canada side; dine at the Clifton House. Next morning are breakfasting at Michigan Hotel, Detroit, with his son, Eugene Smith, eye and ear M. D. Next morning I am seated in the medical chair in his infirmary, and with focus, &c. Dr. Smith says, "Your optic nerve has been injured. You must take the greatest care and caution, and never overtask yourself in any way; you are liable to be stone blind, from which you could never be restored. Have you ever received anything from that 'street nuisance company, &c.' to help you along in your sickness and may be coming want?" "Not one cent." Then (there being several M. D.s present) the whole ball club blow and effects upon me was rehearsed, and it was the unanimous voice of all present "that such treatment as the citizens of North Brookfield, Mass., had thus publicly manifested, deserved the censure and contempt of all civilized humanity." Dr. S.: "My third cousin Hill here will stay there just because her father and mother, and so on, always did. Heavens! I would run from that town if I had nothing more to start with than my first white garment; but Mrs. Hill has got that local 'sticktewitiveness.' She'll stay there 'till they kill her outright." The doctor fitted for me a pair of pebble glasses, which were the first I ever wore.

I returned home after nineteen days roving, tired, but filled with new avenues of thought and pleasant associations and scenes, fitting me to have choice treasures of thought over coming forth to while away this aisle of time. In the fall (November) I attended the Teachers' County Institute, at Ware, Mass., and was entertained in Dr. Richardson's family. Oh, how I love to think over the hours spent in that beautiful home! For every moment there, new life and thought ought to issue. Dr. Richardson took me to the depot in his carriage. He, too, was in manifest anxiety for me, that new remedies might be applied, to aid, if possible, in averting that fearful prospective calamity that may come from that " ball club blow."

The winter of 1873 and 1874 I commenced giving private lessons again, and glad, indeed, was I as I gained strength, that my memory was equal with it as of old. The spring and summer of 1874 I fitted scholars for high school or preparatory for academies from home. In July, 1872, I attended the National Educational Association, in Elmira, N. Y.—my health still very delicate. That meeting of the Association, and its happy reminiscences, are choice treasures in memory's hall. In the winter of 1874 and 1875 I had but three scholars, teaching book-keeping, advanced arithmetic, and a primary scholar. I was present at all public meetings that my health would admit, as reporter ; therefore, reader, I could give you almost verbatim reports of every town meeting during the year and more ensuing. Reader, don't think, for a moment, I entered those public places without escort during said time. I had Tho. Ashby introduce me to J. Lombard, janitor and constable of said town, whom I addressed as follows : " I am correspondent so-and-so, and, wishing for correct statistics, therefore I ask you to give me a seat, and escort me to said platform, and from the same at the close of the meeting," which he acceded to, ever treating me, during said time above mentioned, with the most decorous politeness. As I stated, the old church was re-dedicated October, 15th, 1874, and there followed a general withdrawal from the Union Congregational Church of its wealthiest members—rejoining and joining the First Congregational Church leaving (as report had it) not twenty members.

Chas. Duncan having been heard repeatedly to say, "Freeman Walker was the meanest man he ever knew, etc"; also a remark of a notable gentleman in Southbridge years ago: "If North Brookfield has another man as mean as Sam Skerry, he should think the town would sink."

Reader, my word for it: There are, in said town, at this time, more than twenty men that will beat these two gentlemen " all holler." I almost imagine, my readers, repeating the following epitaph found chiselled on a grave stone:

> "There is a calm for those who weep,
> A rest for weary pilgrims found;
> They softly lie and sweetly sleep
> Low in the ground."

Even J. Duncan, for whom the above mentioned had labored arduously to save for him "said insurance blanket"— he too, in less than six months after, would not purchase meal of said Walker for a length of time, 'giving as a reason " he would not pay for twice the amount of meal he bought," etc. The Duncans were the first to leave the Union Congregational Church, also were the first with the Walkers in its organization.

I think I am through with incidents foreign, as you may think, to the first page preface, but ere this enigma is solved, every different item will find its place.

And for your special amusement I will here pen an inscription from a tombstone in East Tennessee:

"She lived a life of virtue and died of the cholera morbus, caused by eating green fruit, in the hope of a blessed immortality, at the early age of 21 years 7 months and 16 days. Reader, go thou and do likewise."

Died January 4th, 1874, Dr. Porter, physician in the town of North Brookfield for over forty years. Skillful and handsome, thoroughly educated, with quick perception and sensitiveness not to be exceeded, and a staunch friend of mine, in whose family I found rest when in anguish of soul, many times. His many cutting remarks about those who are now in rule in said town often come up before me. And when both of us, laboring in different ways for well-merited work, received abuse in diverse ways, after fully analyzing our maltreatment, he would say, "Mrs. Hill, we shall have to take up with John Nye's motto, 'they will do their d—est, any how—we must let 'em quilt.'" The saying is terribly coarse, but nevertheless true in this town. As my means were limited, Doctor P. had advised me to report for a newspaper, thus paying for some of the mental food I could not live without. It was months before I could make up my mind to do this, and when made up it was brought about in this way. After one of those Young Men's Christian Association gatherings, where singing and reading and repeating are continually held forth till the nervous, and frail minded are in ecstacies of joy such as have been read and talked about, the pulse is high and a glorious revival is aroused. (Readers, don't, I pray, think me trifling with sacred things, for it's far from me; but I have not one particle of faith in that mode of claiming being "new born.") At one of these times some of the evangelists who had been recipients of the rich products in our midst, in getting into the stage (evangelist) remarks, "It's hard leaving after such a bountiful soul-refreshing jubilee as has come of our labor, here."

In the stage, their ecstacies alone were the topic. On the train still comes the same, and more—did you ever meet with such open, liberal hearted people! *That's enough!* I had heard enough; now is my time to give those "evangelists" some real true colors, that color which Omnipotence alone can change, that those church professors have made. Turning my head sideway to them, I said I had not been permitted to enjoy that "soul refreshing." "Do you live there?" "Yes, always; it's my native place, and that of my fathers." "Pray what kept you away?" "Two reasons—the last one, I seldom, or have not been out evenings since April, 1872. At that time I was struck with a ball club upon the right side of my forehead, just above the temple, causing me to have concussion of the brain. My life was in a dangerous state for a length of time, and it was more than six months before I could go down stairs, having to hold my head backward, otherwise dizziness and nausea was the inevitable, and to this day, when weary, the same in less degree manifests itself. " Was it an accidental blow ?" Supposed to be so ; ball playing had been a terror in the streets many, many times for a few years past, or since the great increase of business in the "big shop," and upon that beautiful common front of the First Congregational Church. It had been held by law-abiding citizens a great and dangerous nuisance, as horses had been frightened many times, and balls been thrown through carriage windows, and people's lives before me had been jeopardized, but escaping without serious injury. My injury being so great, I was under direct physician's care for weeks and months before I could work. Some of our respectable citizens called a town meeting in September to do something for me, as my means were limited, and health apparently ruined, my eyesight especially most injured. The town caused printed posters to be placed in legal manner, next day after my injury, notifying the inhabitants that ball playing was prohibited, it being a dangerous nuisance in the street. "Any one *upon any street hereafter playing* said game, whoever violates this warrant notice will suffer the penalty of the law."

Town meeting met as called, and prominent church members were present, many of whom you have spoken of this morning. I will mention a few you have not alluded to, F. Walker, Augustus Smith, S. Skerry, C. E. Jenks, G. C. Lincoln, Eras. Hill, said gentlemen having labored busily during the seven days previous to bring out citizens to vote against my having any remunerative aid. As the town was not holden, the nuisance not being in the street 24 *hours at a time*, and it would not be safe for the town to remunerate such accidents, &c. Thus the meeting dissolved, and but two members of the Union Congregational Church, of which I am member, gave me so much as the cup of "cold water." Mr. De Bevoise and wife watched one night with me ; Mrs. Haston and Emma Lane labored for me, and Mrs. Freeman Walker of the Union Church. "There is something very strange about that,"—I think so, too. Do you think that Christ will say to those soul refreshed brothers and sisters, and the "new called" (it was at this very time "great **outpouring**," meetings were held seven days in the week),

"When I was sick ye administered unto me"? "I know well from your appearance there is some other reason" (*his dander well up*). You will remember I told you I had two reasons, &c., but, sir, your mind being in biblical lore, will you please repeat to me the passage of Scripture where Christ gives an *exceptional rule*. "Madam, you do not manifest a Christian spirit in your conversation." "Perhaps not. Your spirit has changed somewhat within the past few minutes." "Madam, I wish this talk to end right here." "Very well, sir; but I shall avail myself of giving you a verbal looking glass. (All eyes round about us were on us, some highly amused, and two frail sisters that had been taking that "soul refreshing." were in horror). You, sir, are angered as quickly as any one. When you entered the stage your cup of happiness seemed bubbling over, and my opinion is, it was the effects of a good breakfast and night's rest, that your physique is enjoying without break or expense. And without doubt your purse is filled also for such unnecesary 'work' (as you term it) that keeps a hobby for people thus provided for, from performing an act that will meet them for the kingdom. The spirit, look, cut of your jib, shows you are not what you profess. I am through."

At home, next day, at an old acquaintance, whose husband had died not long before, when she came into the room—"You here! from what I heard of you on the cars yesterday, I think the place for you is the insane hospital; and some one who heard what you said, hoped Mr. Evangelist would have you put there." I passed out.

Meeting the president of the Young Men's Christian Association, I said (feeling somewhat excited): "I was going to ask you something about scholars this coming winter that I may keep myself from dire want ere long."

President: "Nobody will care whether you come to want 'ere long' *or now*, if you are going to talk as you did on the cars, &c. (one of the sisters living near him). It is the general opinion you ought to be sent to the insane hospital." What purely *devilish* results comes of these "soul refreshings;" how quick it springeth up! Why the devil's choir those evangelists made here are now *chanting loud !!*

I passed on my way ; said president his way.

But, readers, the above gave me the backbone to go to town meetings, &c., to report for a newspaper, but I have never been to report from those refreshing meetings. I will here state that the First Congregationalist Church attempted to drive out at this time a singer (and one of the best) from the choir; to effect it every singer, forty more or less, left the choir on Sabbath, and such a "high" as that was cannot be equalled. I'll guarantee—do your best. You will remember the year is 1874, and report has it that T. C. Bates made application (or some sign) he would join the Masons, and at the meeting in Brookfield his desire was refused by the "black ball." Bates having the "sticktewitiveness and goaheditiveness" (as Josh Billings tells about) he enters the Queen's dominions, and, while there, is initiated a mason, returns to North Brookfield, "meeting upon the level and parting upon the square." Oh what words of blissful meaning those words masonic are. Thus I hope the reader will follow those above mentioned characteristics, and apply them to the individuals in this book who will show legal heirship to them.

As I have stated before, the town was pledged to have the railroad built and fully equipped with rolling stock for the sum of $100,000, by the glass and crockery ware drummer. He says, if we find, or it can be proved, said railroad, &c., cannot be built and stocked for the sum above mentioned, he should go against it as strong as any other man !!! I will here pen, for the benefit of the reader, "Engineer Keith's report of the railroad route through the Tyler farm, the maximum grade being 116 feet per mile, terminus on the King and Bacheller lot;" but readers, there is a mile rise in said route, "report has it," that is over 300 feet, together with curves, necessary to go through said farm (in order to save a longer cut, and fill through the Kimball worthless hill and vale), thus crossing the road between Hill and Tyler farm ; removing heavy stone walls upon Tyler's farm ; cutting through mowings ; one cut of 14 feet; said wall and part of the earth taken to help fill what was called by the "gang" bottomless mud-hole in the Kimball swamp, and then a fill of 16 feet over soil four and five feet deep, and spoiling valuable building lots, and swallowing up over six acres of said farm, leaving small, not getatable lots, and other portions in trapezums, trapezoids, obtuse and acute angles, in other words, a direct curve line from southeast to northwest, with a rise. that. demands two engines' power to get (with freight, &c.,) through the Tyler farm, in order to have the depot where it is now located for special accommodations of the "big shop" and stores.

Few *business* men *indeed* shall we *get to come* into town to compete with those *stores* and "*big shop.*"

A. & H. Bacheller & Co. now take stock to the amount of $3,000 with the depot located within ten rods of the "big shop." The track crossing at the junction of Elm and School streets, on the main road without expense to said firm, but to lay straight track side of road bed. Which proceedings the County Commissioner came and complied with, April 28th, 1876. Said railroad, the directors dedicated January 1st, 1876. As I had been most insolently refused the right of a disinterested appraisal of my land surveyed, and set off for said railroad, before the taking of the same, necessitating my calling on the County Commissioner in said July, and it pleased said "honorable body," to appoint the 15th day of October, *to view the same.* The railroad work commenced in said July above mentioned in different sections on the Tyler farm, being such that the railroad bed upon said farm was first completed. Thus in August the town road (dividing my land) was filled up seven feet high, depriving me of my direct access to said land to remove my crops, &c. Before the "gang" commenced filling up said road I protested, forbiding its being done to the selectmen, railroad president and directors—repeating to said "Bonum," the statute law of taking and crossing public highways as County Commissioners may direct, &c. Their contemptuous disregard to my every request must be apparent to the reader. I applied repeatedly to G. C. Lincoln, (a Selectman,) to assist me in my effort for legal rights. Lincoln; "What will be the use? you only hurt yourself in the estimation of the railroad men in thus demanding these frivolous exactions of the law, and my advice to you is to hold your tongue." I said, "Mr. Lincoln, how long would you hold on to your tongue if a poor boy in his starving want should take a few cents or pair of stockings from your public store," &c.? Lincoln: " That's a different thing." " Very true sir, and very small importance compared with my wholesale robbery. I know well what your legal investigation of the poor boy, and your sentence to reform school would be."

The work went on, law or no law. The disqualified appraisers labored, figured, offering other claimants different assessments, eventually affecting a settlement with all but five, only a few days previous to the 15th of October; they too called for County Commissioner to appraise, said five, adroitly succeeding with Commissioners in getting theirs appraised through not applying "till past the last watch," the Friday previous to the 15th of October.

Report has it some of the Directors had many interviews with Commissioner, (which I hope will yet be explained,) enabling said body to have profile, perhaps, of parties, &c., through the Directors' microscope.

October 15th, 1875, 9 o'clock A. M.—The County Commissioners met at my residence (by special request), also an eminent lawyer from Worcester on my part and for the town four or five railroad defendants. Prominent among them was advisory " W," one whom I had objected to in writing, before mentioned, as a disqualified appraiser, said railroad company refusing to hear my prayer, &c., thus compelling me to call the County Commissioners. And at this eleventh hour, (the railroad bed having been built through my land weeks previous) the coming of these legal three of the county board, to have F. Walker thrust upon me (as defense for the railroad) in my own house, was, reader, crowning their illegal traffic with outrageous insult. The gentlemen being seated, I addressed them thus: "Gentlemen,—I invited you at this time to my residence for the hearing of my claim for which you have now convened, to avoid the public notoriety which would be had this meeting been in Town Hall." Turning to F. Walker: "I am surprised, sir, at your presence here." Walker : "*I am here officially, madam.*" I passed out into my little room, front (as it were to take on force); coming in, facing the audience, whom I addressed thus: "Gentlemen, F. Walker has for the last few years been my notorious enemy, and an enemy I have reasons to loathe as I would Satan himself, and, gentlemen, if you permit Walker to remain here in my house, I shall leave it at once." V. Taft, chairman of the commissioners, rose and said, " We will adjourn for the purpose of viewing your land taken,&c., and then we will be prepared for further purposes," &c. I just wept. My counsel present said to me, " It's not necessary for you to go down with us, as it rains ; you had better not." Furnishing the three gentlemen with umbrellas, they set off, Walker following.

During their absence, I resolutely bestirred myself preparing every minutiæ for dinner. My table was laid early after breakfast, and all preparations duly made for a sumptuous dinner for said gentlemen. I will also proceed to show my careful preparations by engaging at Chas. Bush's livery stable his best span and coach, to convey said honorable body to and from my residence from depot, as case required, charging said Bush not to fail on their arrival to take the select body as soon as the legal ceremony of calling said meeting to order in the Town Hall, and adjournment to my residence, &c. Saying to Bush, " For all extras, pains, and courtesy, &c., I pledge you I will pay, as well as your regular fee, at the close of said day." Bush agreed to the same. Reader, imagine my astonishment ; some 15 minutes in advance of said time, my bell rang, and at the door I met my counsel's partner, and after due ceremony, I said to him "I had coach and driver waiting for your honorable body when they should come out of the Hall." Esquire: " I saw no such prospect " there ; and soon came the deputized gentlemen *en masse*, *no coach and span !* After all my pre-arrangements, those gentlemen were footing it just like us poor " clod hopping " mortals. Upon return of said legal body, report had it. F. Walker was coming back into the house, whereupon the chairman of said body told " W." he must not. W. says : " Mrs. Hill's *awful temper* in this matter must be subdued."

Commissioner: "I think, sir, your *temper* is decidedly in advance of Mrs. Hill, and I repeat, you must not go again into Mrs. Hill's house." It was then raining hard.

The meeting being in order, I was called on to state my case in full, &c., viz.: In the first place, the straight railroad route would be through Kimball's hill; then it would not have crossed my first mowing—at the most it would take but a small corner off my lower mowing; but to save a deeper cut, and longer fill, through the worthless land above described, they have ruined my first mowing from ever having a building upon it, which I had designed to build; and my plans were near being consummated; and have destroyed two other building lots, which I have been urged repeatedly to sell. My mowing lots have been very valuable on account of the income of grass to cut, which I have sold standing repeatedly for $60, $75 and $85 per year. They have also removed heavy stone walls, and placed as a boundary line, a frail fence, which, as the neighbors and other farming men say, "a good-sized two-year old could get through between the boards, and a medium push would level the whole line." I had also to cut thirty-nine valuable trees. They gave me no chance to remove soil. They also filled up the highway, dividing my land, seven feet, without legal advice and against my remonstrance. The filling as it now stands is dangerous, and it will not be possible to bring up a load without more than twice the power before used.

There are two acres cut off in my lower mowing—being surrounded by three steep, high grades, thus reducing the value of the same in every way. The corner cut off in my first mowing, which is bounded by large walnut and ash trees, I have no access to. Mr. Cram, the builder of the railroad, and Doty, both told me to demand a crossing at this place (notwithstanding the corner contains, as you see, but few rods of land), as they could make there a crossing, the expense of which, to them, would be less than five dollars. I made such demand, and it has been thus far refused.

Also I demanded a wide driveway, crossing from my walnut grove lot over said railroad, leading into my lower mowing; its course to be from the bars that led from the above grove lot in said mowing—said opening having been there more than fifty years. The railroad company refusing this application, you must have noticed the acute angle of mowing left with the heavy wall, and an acre of land there being surrounded, and lying in such shape, is but little better than lost to me. My income from fruit, nuts, grass, &c., has given me yearly from $100 to $125. Now the railroad has laid open for wholesale theft from the "rambling hordes" that work in that "big shop"; the products which are not already in a similar "crib" will be very small in prospective compared with the past. In conclusion, that railroad, as it is built through my seven and a half acres of valuable land, in curve line from northeast to southwest, takes therefrom one and a half acres, more or less.

Commissioner: "What assessment did the directors figure?" Alden Bacheller, hastily replying—"We withdraw that." Commissioner: "What did they estimate?" (I must say, reader, I had an internal ironical smile, being interpreted: you are going to make it the "gauge" for your estimate?) Nevertheless, I promptly informed them, adding: "On my brother's claim at the homestead they made more than double the assessment, and not injured one-tenth as bad as myself." And the doctor's land (I will here state Dr. Tyler is my own full-blooded brother, being eight years my senior in this "mundane sphere") was benefitted many, many hundreds of dollars, as is evident to be seen by all in the work and back boundary it has given him. Readers, do not think my brother's land was overestimated; for it's far from that!!!

I will here pen (the doctor's land was the land I asked for; could I have my choice, &c., in the division of my father's estate. And *bonum magnum* Nye was playing the same game then, that he is to-day against me). I should think Freeman Walker had spent a fortnight, more or less, to adjudicate Lewis Whiting's claim. The different assessment of which I have stated, also stating more than half of said Whiting's land, my father sold him at a price some 20 years since. Being through, the defendants were called upon (said gentlemen had not a word to say). The glance of my eye upon B. M. Nye—with small " pig eyes," was seen by me,—I'll arrange this with the commissioners without audience. Reader, I clearly foresaw his arranged plot. A few words from the legal men present, and said commissioners then adjourned to the Town Hall, at 1 o'clock, P.M., to finish their adjourned meeting of the week previous. . . . I then extended my invitations to said body to have dinner with me, which was ready waiting. The flavor thereof they could not mistake. B. M. Nye thought it not best, and, *of course*, they must refuse on account of so much business, &c. . . . The gentlemen leaving, the lawyer taking the noon train, I verbally regretted the non-appearance of the hired coach for their special conveyance, the reason why I could not conceive. "Therefore, you will please excuse me, for, gentlemen, when I asked you this favor to come to this house for a hearing, and you courteously complied, I forthwith engaged coach and driver to wait on you here and back, and when I learn the reason said coach was not here I will write you. Could those men have stepped out then and there into an anteroom and assessed my land damage, *I have not one doubt but it would have been satisfactory to me.* Reader, Nye knew well the part to play, which will be concluded in subsequent pages.

To make this book more concise, I will here say, the next morning I went to said livery stables, to learn the cause of said engagement not being fulfilled. Said proprietor replying, "I forgot all about it, honestly, and went away in the morning early—had I been at home, it would have come up, and I would have been on hand as agreed." Selah.

You have read of the serpent on the rock; he had crawled off, and was down in the midst—my interpretation of said neglect.

Within a few days I dispatched four letters to the four legal gentlemen interested, informing them it was owing to the *treacherous* memory of said "livery stable man," and his absence from home said day, was the reason, the coach hired was not at their service said 15th day of October, 1875.

Respectfully,

E. R. HILL.

ADJOURNED TOWN MEETING—MARCH 1ST, 1875,
1 o'clock P.M.

Hon. C. ADAMS, Jr., in behalf of the Committee on Finance: The committee chosen by the town on the 24th day of January last, to act with your treasurer in negotiating a loan of ninety thousand dollars, and pay the subscription of the town and the stock of the North Brookfield Railroad Company, beg leave to report they have attended to that service by enquiring into the state of the money market as they have had opportunity. They find the present a very favorable time for negotiating a loan of any kind where the security is good. Money can be had at a lower rate now than at any time for several years past, especially on ·short time, lenders preferring the shortest loans hoping and *expecting* to obtain much higher rates when their short investments mature. The ordinary rates at which savings banks are lending money at a term of years is about seven per cent., but trustees and others knowing changes of trust and sinking funds are letting money $6\frac{1}{2}$ per cent. for a term of years. Just now the supply is greater than the demand at that rate, and it is *possible* the rate may go lower, but a revival of business, or even a prospect of it, would be sure to carry it *higher*. We believe it would be *safest* for the town to secure its loan very soon. We think the rate could not now be over $6\frac{1}{2}$ per cent., and possibly it could be obtained at a fraction lower. This would or might depend on the *time* on which the money is wanted.

The committee would recommend that the town decide by vote how soon they will begin to pay off the loan, and how much they will pay each year, and also vote the rate of interest paid shall not exceed 7 per cent. semi-annually ; also authorize their agents, whoever they may be, to negotiate the loan at an early day, and at the lowest possible rate.

North Brookfield, Feb. 27, 1875.

Respectfully submitted,
CHARLES ADAMS, JR.,
B. NYE,
S. S. EDMUNDS,
Committee.

Voted to lay the foregoing report upon the table, to be taken up at an adjourned meeting.

The Directors made an informal report which was not intended for record or filing. Voted to adjourn this meeting until three weeks from to-day, March 22d, 1877, at one o'clock P. M.

HIRAM KNIGHT,
Town Clerk.

Adjourned Railroad town meeting, March 22d, 1875, at one o'clock P.M.; said meeting adjourned to Monday, April 5th, 1875, at two o'clock P.M. Said meeting adjourned to Monday, April 26th, 1875, at two o'clock P.M.

Adjourned Railroad meeting, April 26th, 1875, two o'clock P.M.—B. Nye, President of the N. B. R. R. Co., verbally reported that the directors are not fully prepared to report today, and made a motion to adjourn for one week, until Monday, May 3d, 1875, at two o'clock P.M.

Voted in the affirmative.

TOWN MEETING, JUNE 7TH, 1875.

At town meeting, June 7th, 1875, the discussions for and against railroads were sharp and bitter, and arguments that the surveyed railroads would cost from one-third to one-half more than the town subscribed, according to the railroad statistics read, Bates blowed off the following:

"If it can be proven that the railroad between North and East Brookfield cannot be built and fully equipped for $100,000, I shall go against it as strong as any other man here. These imaginary bugbears are being brought forward to dampen and prevent this great enterprise from being consummated. I pledge to you, citizens, again, said road can and will be built, fully equipped with rolling stock, within the sum of $100,000." Roars of cheers!!!

Therefore, the motion made by T. C. Bates, That our town treasurer be authorized and instructed to borrow the sum of nine thousand dollars ($9,000), and pay the same to the treasurer of the North Brookfield Railroad Company, as ten per cent. assessment on the subscription of ninety thou-

sand dollars by the town of North Brookfield to the capital stock of the North Brookfield Railroad Company.
Carried by a large majority.
Voted to adjourn to June 14th, 1875, at 10 o'clock, A. M.

ADJOURNED TOWN MEETING, JUNE 14TH, 1875.

Dr. Tyler, Chairman of the Board of selectmen, addressed the citizens as follows:

" The town has saddled a debt on their back of $90,000 for the 'baby,' and most likely before the young one can go alone we shall be called on for one-third or one half as much more for its supplies. I am against my children and children's children—[the doctor has not a child, nor never had]—being cursed with this cumbrous debt; and I move that the town pay said $90,000 in ten annual instalments."

This was a set-back to the railroad men. Angus Smith, J. F. Hebard, Alden and Ezra Bacheller, Timothy Clark, in fact, all of the rabid railroad men opposed Dr. Tyler's motion unrelentingly. Said men proposing to pay only the interest on the loan for five or ten years; after that, $4,500 per year.

The motion of Dr. Tyler was carried.

It is but justice to the parties who have caused this illegal debt to be paid in ten annual installments, four-fifths of whom were against the building of said road (thus most conclusively proving the illegality of the former vote.) The lively lamentation of those railroad men upon prospective taxation was sarcastically amusing to me. Those very men, who are going to be recipients of cheap freight, &c.; and had demanded, with all the force they could bring, that the railroad must be built, or I can't do business here. Oh, where else could be found such "Solomons!"

June 14th, 1875.

Voted, on motion of Hon. Chas. Adams, Jr., " That the treasurer be and he is hereby authorized and directed to borrow of the commonwealth of Massachusetts, or of some other party or parties, on the credit of the town, a sum not exceeding ninety thousand dollars in amount, as may be required by the directors, and to give therefor the notes or bonds of the town, approved by the selectmen, payable nine thousand dollars each year, commencing with the present year and ending with the year 1884, both inclusive, bearing interest at a rate not exceeding seven per cent. (7%) annually, payable semi-annually, for the purpose of paying the subscription of the town to the capital stock of the North Brookfield Railroad Company, made agreeably to the vote of the town passed on the twenty-ninth day of January, 1875.

Voted to adjourn for three weeks from to-day (July 5th, 1875) at one o'clock P. M.

HIRAM KNIGHT, Town Clerk.

Records of town meeting held June 14th, 1875, under a new warrant :

Voted, under Article 2, That the town raise by taxation the present year nine thousand dollars, for the purpose contemplated in the warrant, to wit, to pay the amount which the town authorized the treasurer to borrow June 7th, 1875, and act thereon.

Article 3d. Voted that the town raise by taxation the present year the sum of twenty-five hundred dollars to pay interest on money that has been and may be borrowed to pay for the railroad. Voted to dissolve this meeting.

HIRAM KNIGHT, Town Clerk.

July 5th, 1875.

Adjourned railroad meeting opened at one o'clock P. M. Voted to dissolve this meeting.

H. KNIGHT, Town Clerk.

July, 1875, George C. Cram contracted to build said railroad for the sum of $65,000 (not having the statistics with me, I shall be obliged to omit what I designed at this point) ; therefore said Cram came on with men, horses, and donkeys, locating on my father's farm, now Dr. Tyler's pasture. Next day after their arrival, I called at the Bacheller House, to see said gentleman, and Mr. Doty, his secretary, came forward with a peculiar smirk of readiness to answer whatever I might suggest. Says I, " You are not Mr. Cram, if I have been rightly informed." Doty : " No, ma'am ; but anything you might desire I am instructed to attend to." "Very well, sir ; if Mr. Cram does not choose to come forward, I shall only say to you to say to said Cram, I forbid said Cram, or any of his gang, occupying my farm for the purpose of building a railroad bed, for which he has entered into contract. My land surveyed has not been legally appraised, therefore he must not disturb the same till it is legally in railroad custody." Doty : " Be seated, Mrs. Hill; I will speak to Mr. Cram." " Mr. Cram, Mrs. Hill." " Mr. Cram, I had hoped to have had my land appraised, &c., before your coming; as I have not been able to bring it about, though making strenuous efforts, I shall have to ask you to locate your men somewhere else, the day you intend to commence work on my land." " Mrs. Hill, I have been thoroughly warned that I may expect much trouble with you, your brother, and one or two others ; but I can manage you, and I will give you notice now, unless your crops are removed in such a length of time, I will destroy your crops, regardless of you entirely." " I regret, sir, very much, that you, seeming capable of performing a $65,000 job, should begin it by violating the statutes, thus holding yourself amenable to the law; and, sir, I shall protect myself and rights at all hazard." Thus I left, the railroad fools muttering about and with glistening ferocity, as if they would tear me limb from limb.

I repeated to Alden Bacheller the above. He replied : "Mrs. Hill, I will guarantee you shall have satisfactory pay for your land. Mr. Stone and I have been talking it over, and you may rest assured it shall be made right with you." I left, went to Mr. Leach, and engaged him to cut my grass in both mowings south of the north railroad line staked off, and he proceeded at once to execute my wish—the grass was almost ruinously trampled by the hordes who went over it previously. Mr. Cram did not press matters as in his haste he had suggested, said haste being made by preadvised citizens.

The path being clear some days before, the "posse" ruthlessly stripped me of my best portion of my father's inheritance of this world's estate. Daily I passed among the "gang" at work, gathering items, as fast as matured, for the press. Reader, the overseers, to a man, took my part (so far as appearances tell); thus, when McNulcty began to despoil my land, as directed, he also protected the adjoining land. And never did I receive kinder treatment than from McNulcty and his gang, Cram and Doty leading off in the same way, Mr. Cram saying repeatedly at the table, within two weeks after the above, at Bacheller's house : "Mrs. Hill, instead of being a disturbing annoyance, as he was informed, was the most sensible, used discreet judgment, and made ready for his work better than any one else on the route. We all like her very much."

Thus that peculiar snobbery of North Brookfield was throttled.

Mr. Cram, Doty, overseers and I, are just so yet.

Erastus Hill and Sherman built the culvert under the filling of sixteen feet, said Hill telling his men to draw off some cap stone I desired for my wall, where others had been removed to place under grave stones and monuments from time to time, which he did. I will here relate a little incident to keep up the North Brookfield styles. Those stones remained for a year just where they were laid, being drawn to said place on a new style stone-boat, with heavy yokes of cattle. Being in the grave yard, I asked Perry to put the wall up and make an entrance somewhere else than said corner. Perry: "I want those stones you have stolen and got over in your lot." "What do you mean, sir?" Perry: "Those stones came off the corner, and Tucker says everybody knows it." "And how came they there?" Perry: "Why, you or your men have put them there." "You most contemptible ——, one would suppose those stones of tons weight were piled there as you would so many snow balls; and, sir, I warn you, from what your wife, whom your freaks have located in the hospital, till a new doctor has been placed in said hospital, who has informed you and the public she cannot stay there, not being crazy, the town aiding Perry each time, has told me, I warn you not to remove any more flat, thin stones from my wall for walks, etc. Said wife has repeatedly told me Perry wishes you were compelled to sell that land 'to him.'"

I employed a man for days removing some nice top stones from my half of the wall taken and placed upon my land, beyond the railroad line. And every stone was eventually taken (stolen), and used about fillings in making abutments, which will, ere long, be investigated.

I commenced my brick vault in the cemetery in June, 1875, the work not being completed till fall; said cemented vault being finished like a room—removing my four lost boys from a new hewn-stone tomb built by my late husband in 1858, at homestead. Also I placed the remains of his former wife in the Jonas Bigelow tomb, where she was first entombed. The two men who had been under my employ for weeks—when they had placed my predecessors where I directed, closing said door, repeated, "Susan, farewell!" "Oh, hold me up a minute. My God! if you ain't a hero, there ain't one on the globe."

December 1st return from the county commissioners with $40 in advance of the director's appraisal; no mention made of the bonds I had required, by counsel before mentioned, sending letter at the same time; the bill fee of the commissioners, $21, and costs, to be forwarded at once, adding it would eventually be returned to me. Next mail I informed said counsel I could not comply with his request.

As the commissioners' proceedings were not legally transacted, therefore they must bide their time (with some others), and collect said amount from the town. December 28th, 29th, 30th, I was in attendance at the Massachusetts Teachers' Institute in Boston (of which I have been member since 1867), and there the following legal illumination was given me. (The railroad was going to be dedicated 1st January, 1876.)

"You go home and tell those railroad directors the land and the railroad upon the same is your legal property, and you forbid their trespassing upon the same until they have paid you, or given suitable bonds for the same." I gave said president and directors the above notice when *bonum magnum* NYE replied, "We have complied with all the commissioners' requirements *in full*, and shall do nothing more," &c.

"Sirs,—I give you till eleven o'clock this P. M. to comply with my request above mentioned. Should you fail thus to do, I shall to-morrow morning (which was railroad dedication day) take my chair and seat myself upon my railroad track, and should you attempt to go over the same with the engine, said engine will take me in advance." Alden Bacheller and others whispered with Nye and Bates, Bates loudly asking " How much bonds do you want?" I stating $3,000, naming bondsmen. Bates: "Who told you to ask that?" "Mrs. E. R." A general smile, Nye saying "We will comply." And B. M. Nye and John Dewing came, bringing me the bonds, with one signature, I had asked. I accepted readily, bondsmen John Dewing, Wm. Montague, Alden Bacheller, Dewing and Nye having "invited me to join in the exercises in the morning." I replied, "I have had a chill from wind blowing on me in the cars coming home this eve, and from my feelings now, the inevitable to-morrow will find me too lame for public exhibition." Readers, within forty-eight hours I was under doctor's care, and did not go outdoors for more than six weeks—one of my severe rheumatic sicknesses. During said sickness, B. Nye and G. C. Lincoln came to my house and tendered me the assessments of the county commissioners. They were not accepted. A few more days passed, when they came again, having forgotten to tender the interest; having two or three kinds of moving sticks around me, that is, to aid in moving myself, said gentlemen thought they were not nice enough. I replied, "I have hinted divers ways since the rap with the ball club on my head, the necessity of a gold-headed cane and crutch, and will renew by asking you at this time to see that I have them forthcoming through your special instrumentality," Nye saying, "You shall have them." But they have not arrived yet.

That the readers of this sketch-book may know how the Tyler farm of 200 acres, more or less, has been sold in lots of different measure: First, 80 acres, more or less, to my brother-in-law, Wm. Stoddard, containing heavy chestnut woods; said Stoddard having the same for half of its real value. Father giving the other part to his eldest daughter, said Stoddard's wife. (1845.)

The next parcel of 12 acres, more or less, to the inhabitants of the town of North Brookfield, for the sum of ($1,800) eighteen hundred and some cents; said lessees are to build the wall and ever keep the same in repair without expense to father or heirs. This time brother William died, 22 years of age, almost unfitting father for labor.

The above is Walnut Grove Cemetery; the last portion being most worthless pasture. You will plainly see my east boundary graveyard wall is 56 rods and links.

This was sold after the sudden death of brother Albert (drowned), 20 years of age, at Sturbridge, Mass., where he was studying law with Esquire Hyde.

Esquire Hyde, Dr. of the said town, and five others were in the pond bathing with Albert, when he went down not to rise without aid!!! (1854.)

The next parcel sold to Amos Dean (now owned by Walter Howe), containing 3 acres, more or less, for ($900) nine hundred dollars; said Dean to build the wall and keep in repair this 3 acre lot, is west end of the Tyler farm north of the main road, North Brookfield to East Brookfield; said lot having about 12 rods front. And a neck land back of said 3 acres, father sold to Lewis Whiting, which the railroad had in its bed. (1856.)

Upon south side of said road, father sold to J. F. Hebard, a chestnut wood lot, some 20 rods to 40 rods front, for $1,000, and mowing land back of said chestnut woods, for $100 per acre.

There were six building lots sold off from the Chestnut running back 10 rods, containing about one-half acre each, for nearly $300 each; each lot being in cut of wood condition. Land above described not to be compared with mine ($7\frac{1}{2}$ acres) for locality and products. (1857.)

Dr. Tyler was at this time in Medical College, Philadelphia. I have the exact figures of the above at my home in

North Brookfield, Mass., and by memory, which I have down.

In July, 1875, I was applied to from a parent to instruct Willie that he might be able to enter the High School. His examination papers (after the close of Grammar School), for admission to the above school, were an entire failure. I was surprised, as he had been my scholar, both public and private, with James De Bevoise, some time before.

Thus, having a two-fold interest, I said if the schools in which he had been had not "muddled him," I had no doubt that I could instruct him, making him eligible for above school. Willie Bacheller commenced recitation July 15th, and on the 16th, after recitation, my valuable gold watch (I paid $68 in 1866,) was stolen from my recitation table by John McCarty, 9 years old, who had, during recitation, come to my door and asked to pick some cherries (it was granted). I passed out after recitation with Willie, stopping under the cherry tree; Willie fixing the ladder that the boy might pick me some too (he appeared a pretty boy); I passing about ten rods east of said boy to Mr. Sampson's shop window to *borrow* some implement for the hired man, &c.

Mr. Sampson avers "I did not stop five minutes,"—returning into my own yard, said boy came off the tree, was under the hedge some two rods from the tree. Mrs. Haston's neighbor, in coming to my house, halted at said boy to see what mischief he was at. I said, "Mrs. Haston, please come right along and be seated, while I carry this so and so"—(fifteen minutes had not gone since Willie and I left the recitation room, the watch between the vases of flowers, its invariable place during recitations). I was just going to lock this door and go to my parlor when said boy came with cherries—he could not stop longer—having perhaps a pint. I took a handful, regretting he could not stop as I wished some cherries picked to can, thus engaging the boy to come next day and pick, telling him he should have half, &c.; he agreed to come, 'cause mother wanted cherries. After Mrs. Haston went away—reading, &c., till dark—later, quite dark, thinking to retire without light, as had been my common practice since my "rap"—went down to get my watch and purse. My watch was not there, I said in beating haste, "I have not carried the watch up stairs." All search was vain. I stepped across the road to W. Howe, asked him to go to L. P. De Land, Deputy Sheriff, and have him go for the boy, as he alone had stolen my watch, &c. De Land replied, if the boy had it he would have it in the morning. He would see me and the boy in the morning.

The morning was nearing noon. De Land did not come; I started for him. On reaching his house, Squire Barnes was up in the cherry tree; De Land is from home; Barnes saying to me he was sorry for my loss, and he thought my labor on the Bacheller boy would not amount to anything. It would not be possible to get him into the high school; I replied he will get in if we live, &c. Mr. De Land at this time appears and we go to McCarty; no one in the house; he makes search in vain. De Land takes me home. Mrs. McCarty, whom I knew not, was there intoxicated for cherries. I asked why her boy did not come. "Oh he was sick unto death from eating my cherries, and he was in bed now." Much to the amusement of De Land and to my horor, for my watch was stolen. De Land takes me one side and says, "Get her into the house, it being about 6 P.M., and I will see him at home, as the father will be there." I did as the sheriff said; said sheriff found the father and son. He presented the question to the boy pleasantly, the boy pleasantly answering all questions, also saying there were four or five other boys on the tree and around it. He had not taken the watch, his father crying (said man is always on the grin), saying he told his wife if she sent him to Mrs. Hill's for cherries she'd get him into a fuss and told her not to send him at all. De Land soon returned, telling me "I had got to fix on some other boy, Johnny saying there were four or five about."

I replied, "John McCarty has stolen that watch and no other boy!" "Well, I guess you are mistaken, I did my best to find him guilty, and I could not find the first look of guilt." "That boy has stole and outwitted you." Well, my advice to you is, if you ever have another not to go off and leave it on the table; you admit you were careless." "No, sir, it has thus been left hundreds of times." "The last, once too many." "I will see what I can do." After a sleepless night (making two of them), I rose early, not too early, for Mrs. McCarty was at my door waiting, saying "she felt so bad to think I should send De Land to her house, and accuse her boy of stealing my watch." "Mrs. McCarty, your boy has my watch, and you know it; I have risen thus early to go to Worcester to see Judge Williams, etc. You will be held with your son for my watch, etc. Your boy is young, and perhaps did not realize what a theft he was perpetrating." "He would not steal your watch, he loves you so," and she laid the kisses thick and fast on my hands. "Mrs. McCarty, I respect Father Cronin very highly, and I will let him deal with your boy, and nobody else, if you will go and carry that watch to him and tell him you are most crazed to think Johnny should take it. You hear what I say; carry the watch to Father Cronin before ten o'clock— it shall be hushed up," etc. "Why, I look so to go to the priest; I could not get round at that time." "Oh, yes, go right along." (I think the watch was in her bosom then.) "Mr. Cronin will do just the right thing about it. There is not a man in North Brookfield worthier of respect and esteem than Rev. Mr. Cronin, School Committee," etc. "I know you mean what you say, and I will go and carry it to him right off." Filling her hands with goodies she started blessing me fully equal to an "evangelist."

Morning duties through, my joy made time fly, and ere I was aware it was ten. Now for my mail, and a call on Deputy D——, and find his opinions, and what is best to do, etc. You see I was just teeming with joy. I must play the theatre. I will dress my feet in new gaiters, which will colic my bunions, and there'll be agony unfeigned in my face. Off I started. Deputy D. was at his office, and B. F. De Land and Henry De Land, all three in audience. "I came in, Sheriff, to see what was best to do about Johnny." "I shall not do anything about him, he has not stolen that watch no more than I have." "And, sir, I am just as positive he has." The brothers rather arguing on my side, etc., thus causing the Sheriff to advise me "to go to Jenks, and if he would make out a warrant, I'll go for him." "You have seen Jenks?" "Yes." " Oh, I am in such agony, I just want to screech." "Keep cool, keep cool." "I cannot, I am in perfect misery; and I am going up to see Father Cronin and get his advice." " I should advise you not to go near him, of course you will do as you please." "Yes, I shall compass heaven and earth if that watch is not forthcoming. Good morning."

At the priest's, Father Cronin, seeing me coming, meets me at the front door-step, with coat in hand, saying, "I was just going to come down and see you, and bring what there is left of your watch." Seating me in their parlor, he returned, bringing my once watch, all torn to pieces. My agony was then something beside my feet. He says: "It shall be replaced in value equal to your loss," &c. " Oh, Father Cronin, why is it everything connected with me is tortured—thus torturing me in every devisable manner." " 'Those the Lord loveth He chasteneth." '· I want longer breves between " chastenings.' " Turning round, he soon appears : " I will see the boy ; his mother will send him to me this P. M. * * I will take the watch and show it, and then you will take it and see if it can be fixed." " Yes." I called on Sheriff D—— and showed what was left of the watch, both brothers being present. Mrs. McCarty came to my house in the afternoon, when we effected a settlement. Mrs. McCarty paying $40, giving her note for $18, payable on or before the 1st of September, 1875, and what remains of the watch is now to be kept with dead baby's clothes.

Next day after settlement she came, saying "W. H.," &c., " has told her to go and get that watch ; she will be arresting your boy any time she can show that torn up watch, and if you had not been a d——n fool she never would have found it, and the whole town was glad she had lost it. Go, get that watch from the mean thing." Thus she became furious as a madman, set on solely by drunken, low Yankees. Thus she raved for a time. A few Sabbaths after I was in the graveyard, and Foster and Jenks met me, both 'ving a leering look at my chain, as if saying, "She has the watch on." I had my locket on. Report had it that Foster, constable, had stated he would rather give $100 than have me find it, and Con. Bliss said I had not lost my watch. Bothwell joined the young insurrection against me.

In due time I, with Con. Hunter, called at Mrs. McCarty's, the little girl admitting us in an entry very small. Mrs. McCarty, with bread knife in hand, flourishing it, locked the door, scaring Hunter as pale as death. I said, "Timmy, take that knife from your mother or I shall." He did so. I told her what I came for. "She never would pay me a cent; it was a lie I had told, saying her boy had stolen my watch; every body knows you are a liar, and mean." Timmy let us out, getting the key away from his frenzied mother by a *ruse*. The constable saw me home, and said he never was so frightened in his life. I was in fear, but kept my presence of mind until I was out. I was so weak I could hardly stand. That drunken woman went calling same evening for Foster to arrest me for disturbing the peace, and report had it I was arrested by said Foster, who was in glee over her, charging her never to pay another cent on the watch, and the $40 is all I have received from her, and not a word from Hunter or myself to cause the above report. I have applied to Deacon Montague of the "big shop" firm to try and make said parties pay the remainder. Montague: "I think you and I had better let the law have its course." C. E. Jenks is going to have me taken for compounding a felony. Reader, I do not propose to apply to the law for justice, and expect to get any through such agents. Neither shall I let them or any one be getting from me (after losing my watch) whatever they desire to strip me of, because I spot the sinner.

"Charles Duncan had a clerk who abstracted $1,200 from his store drawer, and he had it refunded with interest. Said money had been banked as fast as drawn," &c.

No compounding felony in that case. That "compound" belongs to Mrs. Hill in getting the ruined watch, if she can.

Three days gone. Willie B. is in recitation, and we know when the hour is gone by the town clock striking.

I gave him twenty-eight lessons. He entered the high-school; Mr. Clay, teacher, saying, "among the first examinations he was the poorest of any scholar examined in the school, and now he enters bearing the best examination of any scholar."

Two young misses entered through my instruction notwithstanding the mob's efforts to keep some vile contumely of their own inheritance going round.

"The more eminently virtue shines, the more it is exposed to persecution."

NORTH BROOKFIELD TOWN MEETING, MARCH 1st, 1876.

T. C. Bates now cautions his "dupes" as follows : "The great question to-day with the voters and tax-payers is, with how small an amount of money can the town meet its obligations the coming year?" Our rate of taxation for 1875 was $19.25 on $1,000, and the money raised by the town was as follows :

Schools	$7,000
Support of poor	1,500
Highways, bridges and sidewalks	4,000
Interest on town debt	1,000
Contingent expenses	3,000
New hearse	1,000
Memorial day	100
Railroad	9,000
Interest on railroad debt	2,500
	$33,100
Amount of State tax	2,820
Amount of County tax	2,317
Overlayings	840
	$38,077

Total valuation of town, $1,845,675.
Rate of tax on $1,000, $19.25.

"Now, the question is, how much of this amount can we do without in 1876? Can our schools be maintained with any less sum? It is thought $500 may be deducted from the appropriation of last year, and our schools fully kept up to their present high degree of excellence. And there should be $1,500 less on the highways and sidewalks. The payment of $9,000 of the railroad debt must be provided for, and about $5,000 interest on the balance, making $14,000 to appropriate for maturing railroad obligations.

Now, if our town officers will give their services for a few years, or for one year, that would help us out very much; but if they cannot, or rather will not, they really should be willing to work as cheap as some officers in neighboring towns. But they can all afford to donate their service for one year, at least, especially if the present officers are re-elected to-day, and every advocate or friend of the railroad enterprise should work earnestly to reduce all expenses in our town affairs. A very few of our citizens, and the most conspicuous of the few advocates (and having no family to receive the benefits of more school room) are very desirous of adding another burden of four or five thousand for another school house in the center. Now, we can make our present accommodations suffice for a few years more, and this can be easily done if parents will not be so anxious to get their children out of their way and under the teacher's care as soon as they can walk alone and find the school-house.

Sketch or Two of Town Investigations at this March Meeting Day, 1876.

Bates comes forth a saviour for the interest of the town. Therefore a general look over the town proceedings of many years of G. C. Lincoln, merchant, treasuryship. His bonds have never been legally sworn, &c., some bondsmen not knowing they were held as bondsmen, showing up the town had never received, according to reports, any interest on money during the eight years, more or less, of said Lincoln's service, &c., as town treasurer. G. C. L. said there had never been any to put at interest. True, of course. And thus bringing about Bates' prearranged plan. That as fast as money of such an amount should be in hand, it be deposited in some bank, that interest should be accruing for the benefit of the town (instead of treasurer). Therefore, a new town treasurer was elected to office, bondsmen all sworn publicly, and that car just started for the first time right. Next—

S. BOTHWELL, COLLECTOR AND TREASURER OF TAXES, NORTH B.

His bondsmen, too, had never been legally sworn, &c.

More than all that, Bothwell had been collecting interest from the poor " clod-hoppers " on their great sacrifice tax for four years, more or less, amounting to, it must be, hundreds of dollars, and not one cent ever went into the treasury. S. Bothwell rose looking lanker than you could imagine any one, except Uriah Heep, and said " he was going to pay it, and had always intended to, every cent." Of course that was all right. Reader, he had had beside $300 or $350 per year for collecting said taxes. These being the two worst leaks in the town purse, the rest will not be mentioned.

April 10th, 1876.—The directors of the North Brookfield Railroad Company reported. The present board of directors was chosen at a meeting July 3d, 1875, in selectmen's room, and there have been stockholders' meetings twice since, convened by request of the directors, November 11th, 1875, to authorize the directors to lease our railroad when done to the B. & A. R. R. Co.; and on February 7th, 1876, to ratify and adopt a code of by-laws for the company directors— Bonum Nye, Freeman Walker, Alden Bacheller, Liberty Stone, John B. Dewing, Warren Tyler, W.H. Montague, Geo. C. Lincoln, Theodore C. Bates.

I will give costs of building N. B. R. R. You will remember it was to be built, fully equipped with rolling stock for $100,000.

By amount paid on construction account		$78,171	22
" " "	engineering	3,485	44
" " "	incidentals	816	02
" " "	land damage account	15,390	47
		$97,863	15

North Brookfield, Mass., 1875.—Total valuation, $1,845,675.00.

Total number of inhabitants as returned by State enumerator, 3,748.

Town pays Boston & Albany Railroad, $2,000 per year for lease of rolling-stock, which is the simple interest of $33,333⅓; said sum added to $90,000 amounts to $123,333.33⅓. $123,333.33⅓ divided by $1,845,675.00=quotient, .06⅔ cents. Therefore the town is actually taxed .06⅔ per cent on a dollar to make a dozen men wealthy.

When the town voted to raise 5 per cent. of her valuation, there were but forty-eight hours more, when the die would be cast, and then 3 per cent. of her valuation alone could be raised. A wayfaring man, though a fool, can see from the above that we are taxed 6⅔ per cent. The town subscribed to become an associate before the said law was made statute. If I remember right it became statute the May following, January 29th, 1875. The defect in the above proceedings, if allowed to stand without investigation and prohibition, is demoralizing to the nation.

Should a suit in equity be brought to recover taxes thus illegally paid, the result will affect the destinies of unborn numbers for weal or woe.

Again, if courts will sustain towns in borrowing money without limitation and distinction, in direct violation of the statutes, what is to prevent every town in the government from becoming bankrupt? Thus I argued, and could I believe those railroad men enacted what is their mind, I should have been "squelched" from mortal view. After the town meeting I went into Bates' path.

What meaneth it, $98,000 swallowed up and no rolling-stock? Bates: "I have heard enough of your blab sticking round here; you would be glad to have folks think you literary, your inch long pieces in the paper. There ain't a person in town but what hates the sight of you!" "They don't hate the sight of my income and land that is taken and made a sinking fund to benefit the 'big shop' and stores. Every time you or any one else rides in those cars over my land, I am contributing largely for their every ride," &c. "You a sinking fund? As though you had money! The town has offered you ten times the worth of your land, but you will fight, and I will tell you now, when you get through your suit for damages, you won't have money enough left to buy the grub for your next meal."

April 28th, 1876.

The County Commissioners, in session at North Brookfield, I suppose them to say to railroad directors: we could not have advised you better in the crossings of these roads than you have done, and we are highly pleased with the crossings thereof, &c. But their ardor was cooled when I appeared, presenting a letter to Commissioner Brown, saying, "You will please to attend this day to the complaint within" (I have not the copy, it is in North Brookfield). Mr. Brown: "We may not have time." "I wish you to comply this day with my request," &c. I then passed on my way. Report has it Brown opened the letter, smilingly, passed it to F. Walker: "I can't read that." He took said letter, looked it over, passing it to Bates: "If you can read bad spelling and writing, try that letter—ha! ha!" Bates read aloud said letter without hesitation, to the great edification and joy of the bystanders, who said, "Mrs. Hill had him!"

In said letter was a complaint of the road, in which the railroad had made a rise of seven feet—the north descent being fifty feet, the south eighty feet. Said commissioners on the 2d of December, 1875, notified the town to grade said filling 100 feet north and 150 south. Said commissioners proceeded to view the same. I was there. The commissioners asked if any one could tell them the grade ordered by them? December. Dumb silence. Nye, Walker, Bates, &c. I have seen intended ignorance before. But I will inform you. Some of the selectmen and railroad directors have told me the road was complete, and nothing more to be done, &c. And your orders are upon the court records 100 feet north and 150 south. Mr. Bigelow says to the directors, "you make that grade at once." Oh, those countenances! I see them now as then.

Within a month the Boston & Albany Railway were dumping sand upon said filling, leaving it again 80 and 120 feet. I dispatched another letter to said directors, demanding completion, as legally ordered.

McKay contracted and finished out said work. In doing the same they stole all the stones that lay in heaps upon my own land, placed there by my hired men when the railroad was building; Nye telling said men to pile some upon the wall. Readers, please notice the *trespass and stealing.*

The trespass of rocks being placed upon my mowing by Carter, who made the first grade; said overseer being the only one that was a complete tool for the directors—McKay bringing up the rear. Said Carter, men and horses, were kept by Mr. Tyler a length of time; said Tyler losing $260 by them.

The commissioners compelled the directors to make my lower crossing as petitioned, but in the first mowing, it is not granted.

April 1st, 1876.—Bates has in the *North Brookfield Journal,* viz., "The railroad company is virtually the town. It is a question in which all our people take a deep interest, and are firmly united in the sentiment that the awards are all sufficient, and every effort to make the compensation larger should be contested to the last degree. But it is hoped these dissatisfied claimants do not want a legal contest for the benefit of lawyers and the disadvantage of their own neighbor friends. But if it must come, the almost unanimous feeling of our citizens is, that it must be opposed to the furthest extent."

April 28th, 1876.

I wrote to the directors to grant me a hearing before three of their body, specifying them to see if there could be brought about a railroad settlement. Their reply to me was: "When the other four are settled, then we will try you."—SELAH.

May 1st, 1876.

To our *patriotic, public spirited* citizen, Charles Kittridge, belongs the honor of having first brought his unsettled claim for land damages, before the courts. Since the last issue of the *Journal,* the officers of the Railroad Company have been summoned to appear at Fitchburg, at the June Term of court.

Mr. Kittridge's case against the N. B. R. R. Co. is No. 1052 on the docket, and, of this number, *over* 850 have not got even called, and the best authority obtainable says it cannot be reached in much less than two years, and then it may take two years more to decide whether Mr. Kittridge's wood lot is worth $150 per acre, as we have offered him, or only about $40, as good judges of honest men have appraised it. We are sorry Mr. K. is so determined to throw his money into the basket he has selected, and cause the railroad officers so much trouble and annoyance, though the company may not have to pay HIM so much by a hundred dollars, yet the court expenses will consume it, and that was their opinion when the liberal offer of $150 was made him. If this money at *interest* will not *amount to more* by the time this case is settled than he will get after paying his lawyer's fees, costs, and all other expenses attending the controversy, we are very much mistaken, and our citizens generally will feel as though our respected public benefactor should have some slight token of their appreciation and respect for his noble generosity, and probably the hat will be passed around to get the money to pay his bills after he has been beaten in the courts. At any rate, the respect they will always have for him will be of great value to such sensitive, appreciative persons as both Mr. and Mrs. K. have shown themselves to be. Have we any more such people in our town? Time will tell.

May 27th, 1876.

Burglars are still on the scout in North Brookfield. They have made several attempts to enter residences within the past few weeks. They tried again, about one o'clock, at Mrs. E. R. Hill's residence. Their noise awoke her, and her alarm given to the neighbors drove them away. Liberty Stone had evidence of their trail upon his premises the same night. D. Whiting, A. Bacheller, Blood, and DeLand went to Mrs. Hill's aid.

Before forty-eight hours were gone a vile report was heralded to me, as my sayings in my fright. Where did you hear the loathsome, obscene—oh, horror! oh, my God, why dost thou not cause their tongues to cleave to the roof of their vile mouths? "They said you was as crazy as a bed bug." "Tell me at once, who is bearing that vileness to be bandied through that 'big shop'?" "Wilder Dean, Eddie Bacheller, both were telling of it." My hat was on my head, quickly. "Keep cool, and give them what will live and be to their benefit." I was soon in said market, saying, "Bacheller, a vile slang is being reported, and you with Mr. Dean are said to be reporters; did you coin what you told in presence of Mr. ———?" "No, I didn't; I have heard more than forty tell of it." "Please name one.". "I can't; there was more than twenty last evening; I did not notice— it was the general laugh." ".Will you please tell me one in this market last evening that did not join the rabble." "I shall not say anything more." W. Dean's answer same. "You both are legally held as coiners of this vile report, verifying the adage, 'out of the abundance of the heart the mouth speaketh;' I have found who the author of this vile talk is, and I leave you with disgust and contempt."

Reader, that is a perfect representation of the style of eight-tenths of the citizens of North Brookfield, Massachusetts, the modern population.

Patrick Kellogg's residence had the same kind of a call at the bed-room window, both husband and wife seeing and recognizing the man; as report has it, Bothwell, and selectman, and the family think it best to hush it up. So much for statutes and officers, to mete out justice *to whomsoever they will.*

As I was returning home I thought it best to tell Mr. A. Bacheller what came from said market, and the authors, when weeping, Bates tunes up, as he comes into the store, "Miss Hill, you got ready to take the commissioner's award." This is your time to taunt also. I left the store without purchase. I will here state I have twice written A. H. Bacheller & Co., of the "big shop," offering to sell him all the land cut off below the north side of the railroad, giving them the commissioner's award, &c. Not one word; so much for that, and my effort in the same way to other interested parties has received the same attention. The award rendered is a song composed with the injury and income the railroad has taken for their special benefit.

My land has been set on fire four times by the engine, burning once all over north of railroad bed. Three times I was notified, and with help extinguished it.

I was told by the engineer before the railroad was complete, after the first burning (I was at Worcester at this time of the fire), "it would be impossible to have a building upon my two acre lot, owing to the great power required to come up and around the curve." My loss is great. My cherished plans are dashed to the ground. My best part of my livelihood taken for a sinking fund for "big shop," a few stores, and, as report has it, free-ride passengers.

I have repeatedly asked them to remove posts, &c., upon their five roads, taken as they are set irregular, acknowledged by one of the best engineers from a city. "They shall do nothing about it." Said engineer proving, in his survey, more land in railroad bed than the profile affirms. I said to the engineer, "How shall I remove those posts—the directors will never have it done?" "I should take an axe and knock them over."

Reader, I will commence again, July, 1876. As I have told you, of owning by heirship, seven and a half acres of land, which the North Brookfie'd Railroad ruins in many ways, the income of which has been stated heretofore, selling my grass standing, etc., this July, not an offer (bear in mind reader, the railroad ring are vigorously running their *underground railroad* to shut off my income, and thus to have an argument which will soon be related). I bestirred myself to sell my crop of grass to A. B. C. without avail; finally hearing that John Sherman, whose wife is second cousin of mine, and a very weak minded lady, had moved into the village in absolute need of assistance, being a coal truck driver, and formerly living with his bachelor brother-in-law (Peniman Tyler, great singing teacher), whom report says Sherman had run through "Penn's" property, and his name held also for $1,000. Mr. Daniel Whiting advised me to get Sherman to cut my grass, on conditions, etc. Next morning I started for Cork to find John; before I reached that isle, I met John Sherman, and I appealed to him for a trade, etc. "Oh, I am tired to death of haying—I have all I can do, and more too. You could not induce me to cut it, if you'd give me the whole crop."

Before I reached my home, I met Captain D. W. Lane, he saying if I did not succeed in selling my grass—he would, after his haying, see it was harvested, &c.; oh, this pulling up-hill, all done by that old railroad; my two-acre mowing was a highway for six months. I shall not have half crop anyhow; thus I soliloquized. Anecdote—"A certain *gentleman* being asked, why it was he talked so much to himself." "For two reasons, sir: First, I like to talk to a sensible person; Second, I like to hear a sensible person talk. Now, bide your time." 26th July, in comes neighbor: "Well, John Sherman has concluded to cut, or bought your grass." "I had not heard so; did you hear who made the trade?" &c. "I heard Belding say so; he wanted to sell Sherman some hay to pay him for cutting his, as he had to feed his horses without being asked at noon; Sherman boldly pitching in his cart for their night, want, &c. Sherman hain't a forkfull of anything for those two horses; one is Penn's and the other Ben. Dean's." "I'll just start for that driver, and see if I can't rescue him from further robbery more, thus accomplishing a two-fold object, helping myself and cousin John S., too." At John Sherman's door, he shouts, "Come in, Mrs. Hill." "Please excuse me for this untimely call. I have just been told you had bought my grass, ha, ha! haven't you got your haying done, nor haven't you bought it; ha, ha!" "I'll tell you, Mrs. Hill, I'll be down to-morrow morning, and buy your grass. Less trade now." "You may cut it at the halfs, or I will sell it standing $12½ per ton." "I will give you $12½ per ton, and pay in thirty days." Agreed. "Mr. Sherman, I want two tons of coal put into my house and barn the earliest time possible; can you deliver as before, for me?" "Yes; and will put it in within thirty days, and the balance as before." "Agreed." That man cut two mowings, and housed in the next two days, amounting to $17.62, what had been sold standing, in 1874, for $85, to John Rusk.

I informed G. H. DeBevoise of Sherman's proceedings, etc. Said DeBevoise told me he would see said gentleman, that if I would not enforce the law he would bring about payment. Sherman is a church member in regular standing.

Mr. DeBevoise did advise him to pay me as report has it. Not one cent have I received yet. I have also appealed to Deacon Haskill, Deacon Thurston, Deacon Porter and Deacon Montague, said deacons officiating under G. H. DeBevoise, Lewis Whiting, Walter Howe, members.

Deacons Porter and Montague, (very wealthy) both being brothers-in-law to Sherman by marriage, say nothing of that "double distilled brotherhood." They, hearing my complaint, said: "We will investigate, etc." Due time I asked them the result of their investigation. Deacon Thurston said: "He has offered to pay you," etc. He has used those words and nothing more, gentlemen. I caused Esquire Barnes to write to him to meet Mrs. Hill at his office such an evening (waiting for Sherman to do his day's work and have supper) to settle a claim for hay, etc., and to bring the bills of the same. After waiting nearer two hours than one he came, saying he would pay for the hay he had, but he should not cut my garden nor draw my coal. "Very well, sir, I will take the money." Barnes: "Sherman, give me the weight bills." Sherman opens them with rapidity, and throws them on the table. "There you have 'm." Barnes begins figuring; before he could complete the same, Sherman says: "Barnes, here is $20," (I looking and noticing every move—he had folded a bill in his hand, clinching it tight—Barnes nor I had no means of knowing what it was but Sherman's word,) adding, you take pay. Barnes: "No, we will square it all up in a minute." Sherman starts for the door, saying: "Barnes, I'll be in to-morrow and see you." "Mr. Sherman, I wish this settled to-night, I cannot come here to-morrow. If you have a $20 bill, show it. You have not, nor don't intend to pay one cent." He fiendishly grins and says: "Barnes, I'll see you to-morrow."

"Mrs. Hill, I think he will come in." Sherman was down stairs by the time the above was uttered. "Mr. Barnes, did you see anything to make you know Sherman had $20?" Barnes: "No, not at all." When Sherman landed at the foot of the stairs he volunteers as follows: "I've just offered Miss

Hill $20, to pay for her hay, and she won't take it. When I offer it again you let me know." Into Chas. Duncan's store, and repeats the same, at Tim. Clark's and W. Dean's and Sargent's fish market. Next morning he calls on Barnes and demands the weigh-bills; and Barnes gives them up, saying he wasn't ready to pay, and more than that he should not pay Miss Hill till he got ready. In P. M. I called on Barnes, and he stated the above, adding, sometime in the course of time, "Sherman is such a hard ticket you may get a chance to collect the same." Reader, that is all the kind of offer from Sherman I have had. But Sherman received from me kindly aid while getting said hay, besides his horses living upon it both days. The stolen hay lasted Sherman till the law, enforced by others, took the horses out of his barn, and said hay not quite consumed he boarded a Frenchman's horse to finish the same. And the church members had their coal drawn $1 per ton, by Sherman, and other servile labor proportionately cheaper, saving said men dollars, more or less, by Sherman having my timely hay.

Sherman, report has it, is often intoxicated, though he has signed the pledge recently—a fearful specimen of untruthfulness, yet a member in regular standing in DeBevoise's church. I just said to DeBevoise, about three months since, one Thursday, before communion, "I would like to have you remind Sherman, as *he is, with you*, about to commemorate the dying love of Christ, while his mind may be in a tender state, Mrs. Hill (widow) needs the pay for her hay very much." DeBevoise: "Yes, 'em."

Readers keep tally of names.

In August I attended the Teachers' County Institute at Milbrey, Mass. North Brookfield was well represented, it being the County Institution. I think I am the only one belonging to National, American and State Teachers' Institutes in N. Brookfield.

I went to the Centennial alone in November, 1876. On reaching New York I crossed over to Brooklyn, to Rev. Henry W. Beecher's, hoping thus suddenly (without cards or previous letters) to find Mrs. Catherine Beecher, but doomed to disappointment, seeing only Mrs. H. W. Beecher; Miss

Beecher absent and in very poor health. Returning at once to New York, Broadway, calling at American Institute, of which I have been a member, to get my certificates and photograph. And in the same block, in Browne's Phonographic College, I learned and paid for two lessons in phonography, Mrs. Browne saying I had made more proficiency than many students in college in three months. Seeing right there, were Fowler and Wells, that old acquaintance Fowler examining my head in public, in North Brookfield, Mass., in 1847. Said gentleman giving me a wonderful cranium, of course gave me audacity to renew acquaintance, and see what he thought thirty years had added to the above capacity; I met only Wells, and talked with him an hour or more. I ought to have said while in Browne's college, Mrs. Browne invited me to call with her at Dr. Holton's genealogical compiler, where we dined about 7 P.M. I think it was the Astor House, Mr. and Mrs. Browne introduced me, paying my bill, in advance for me. The house was on the European plan. Reader, have patience with me about names. Remember my guide books are at my cottage home. The above mentioned places I hope to call at ere I leave this city, notwithstanding my outside apparel is poor indeed. But I guess they will give me a hearing. Now off for the Centennial; at the mammoth depot, at the right office, I presented my ticket. "The Bound Brook train has just gone (not ten minutes); you will have to wait about two hours, &c.; go to that further seat" (pointing to the last door). I went and stayed *some long time* before another passenger came for said train, but just before starting hundreds packed there. When the gate opened I was *first*, and the *first* to show my ticket to the officer stationed. He looked it over, "Madam, you're all right, go to the last car on this second track." I demurred. "We begin to fill up at further end," (pointing). I did just as I was told. The car none too good for four-footed beasts. Nevertheless, it was soon packed, not an extra seat for the many more searching.

All aboard—we are off. In due time conductor takes my ticket. "You are on the wrong train, madam; you must pay me so and so." "That I shall not do, sir. I have been waiting two hours for this train. I was told at the ticket office to take such a seat at such a gate, which I did; not another individual there at the time. When the gate opened, I was first to give my ticket to the officer in charge there, and he told me I was all right, and directed me to this very car I am in, sir," "That's so," came from three or four I was next to.

Conductor: "That's nothing to me; I must have that fare, so and so, or you must get off the train."

"I shall not pay you one cent, sir. You see here, sir; my ticket, bought at North Brookfield, Mass., to Philadelphia and return. And, sir, I am in this car by officers directing the traveler. You can stop the train and put me off, the result of which will be a legal investigation of the same."

Conductor: "Madam, I'll look this up." On he goes.

Reader, there was no other one in this car to be *ousted*. I began thinking aloud—an old habit. That officer thought me a countrywoman. Now for some extra change, arranged for before; but the "sharks" got hold of the wrong "greenhorn" this time. A general snicker, and louder, roused me to know I had some audience. At the same time a gentleman coming to me said, "Madam, they got hold of just the right one this time. Permit me to render you a little assistance at this time." "Thanks—please investigate with the conductor." In due time the said gentleman returns with the conductor, bowing and taking his seat. Conductor said, "You can stop at Newark. Wait there till four o'clock. I will see you are sent to the depot for the Bound Brook train," &c. "Thanks—what time shall I reach Philadelphia?" Such a time in the evening! The train stops. That gentleman (minister) rose, took my linen bag, &c., with conductor, and helped me off the train —conductor ordering the hackman to convey *this lady at once* to such a depot for Bound Brook train. Minister (for he looked and acted just like one called of God), shaking hands, said, "I wish you success and much pleasure the rest of your journey."

Conductor. "I the same." And they are off.

Here, in Newark, I am stopped, not by my carelessness, but by man's greed to get the dollar without giving an equivalent. But I will see and learn from every crook and corner round about. I'll get so much into my head, that land sharks can't get hold of. On the train, and I am seated with a stately, richly and well designed dressed lady, whose white hair and general look spoke sixty years and more. We readily engaged in conversation, and the unfolding brought out her special troubles, her rich grounds and fruits corporations had taken to build such, and such men in business, so, and so ruining the looks of her inherited residence, and the one place she had lived in previous to her husband's death taking thousands and rendering for the same a nominal sum. "I could not bear to stay there. I sold out, but have ever been sorry I did sell my home. You and I are too far advanced in life to sell out and rove like these pilgrims, who stay a year or few months here, and then off. And too many seek such a life to rob their living from the honest industries of others." As she is about to leave the train— "You and I have met, as it were, strangers in a bond of sympathy, and as I am the eldest let me say to you, from my experience, keep your home unless driven out by fiends, with which the world so abounds." A shake. Gone.

Another lady coming to me, who came to the depot at Newark, and had heard the conversation more or less, advised me to get off at next station with her, and there await (she would wait with me, as her home was there) till I could take a train for Bound Brook. And she would advise me to stay over night there and rest, if I was near as weary as I looked. The hotel at Bound Brook was just across the street from depot. A nice house, reasonable prices, and of the best in every way for your need. Soon I am on the train, in the seat in front of me is a little boy, four years of age, bright and beautiful. We made quick acquaintance, and I soon had several kisses from his sweet cheeks. His aunty with him says he is a great pet every where, and living in a hotel gives him a great deal of presence for his age. I am directed to such a hotel. It is this boy's father's. Boy—"You going home with me?" The father comes from smoking car. Thus strangers form acquaintance. My bed, my food was the very best, and more by far than that was the parlor hospitality and sociability, that was so much in the example of the life our Saviour gave us, the fruits thereof I was the recipient. I regret I cannot give the name. It was a democratic house, and a rallying open air meeting was held in front of said hotel, every word of which I could hear in my room. Their truths uttered, they helped to lull me to sleep. Next morning, about 8 o'clock, I was on right train for Centennial grounds reaching there about noon, coach conveying me to Atlas hotel where I had a room till I left. Friday about 7 A. M. I commenced explorations, before an hour had gone after my arrival upon said grounds, and sped my way this way and that, unconscious of people but things. How soon dark! I had not thought, how shall I get back to the Atlas hotel again? First, inquiry—"such a hack, such a way," &c. I was directed as the best way into a street off the grounds (just the worst way), and by indefatigable perseverance ran on. At last those long dining halls came in sight. My thinking out loud—that's the Atlas hotel kitchens. "Are you, lady, wishing to go there?" So much for thinking out loud. "Yes." "We are going there—we have stopped there the past week." The parties speaking were two women hanging on one man. Very suspicious looking to me. Soon in the great reception room, and clusters of mortals were round the tables in every direction. As I aimed to go direct for my linen bag, &c., "Do stop here a moment, lady, you look as though you could not get up stairs without help," &c. "I am very weary, (the man and other lady going in different directions—from the moment that woman spoke to me I knew they were pickpockets, as if it were spoken from heaven), but fully competent to do all I have to do." Lady: "You here alone?" "Yes." "That lady and her husband that have gone to supper—" "They have supper in different directions." A cooler. "I was going to say, I room alone next to theirs, and I would like to have you room with me. We both show we have no abundance of money." "My room is engaged and paid for." "Pray what number is it?" "None of your business!" I went to the baggage office corner. I pointed out the lady to a gentleman, telling him her conversation. Says porter, "I think she is the very one last week we suspected or alluded to—go, look, Joe." A waiter, going up stairs to my room with my bag, &c., after bringing me refreshment, informed me a man had just found his watch was stolen. "Am I secure in this horse stall?" Laughing. "Yes."

My rest was poor; my gas-light revealing the bedbugs around the hole of the gas-pipe, in boards and ceiling. I finished a newspaper almost in killing them as they entered, with their gore marking, by my handy designs, Palestine, so deftly plotted on the Centennial grounds. Next morning I was on the ground about the first, swiftly viewing in the main building; I came to the manger where the Saviour's horned ox was produced, and wise men of the East, &c., were to be seen. I lingered in reverie. A simple mind, beautiful in outward dress, spoke to me: "Do you suppose this is really the stable Christ was born in?" As I looked at her, this passage came in my mind, "Answer a fool according to his folly," &c. "Oh, yes; the mode of conveyance is such now-a-days we can transport anything, of whatever name, or nature," and passed on with disgust, that a young woman that could put so much dry goods about her, and be such an ignorant fool—thus my profound reverie was broken. The crucifixion next held me long; and, reader, I see that statuary this moment as plain as my pen and paper; and "My Imprisonment in the Felon's Cell," by Bothwell, was so parallel, the thought of which makes the blood rush to my cheeks as if to burst the skin. Another frail voice says, "Have you seen what I call 'Niagara Falls?'" "No, what do you mean?" "Oh, where all the engines are pouring water." That 'Niagara' was no more to be compared to that stupendous, awful grandeur, than so many squirt-guns. Nor Corlis' wheel was not so much of a sight to me as "Haskell's last-factory wheel," seen in 1837.

One more ecstacy: "Have you seen the 'Butter Image?'" "Yes." "Was it wonderful?" "No; all that is wonderful to me about it is the chemical principles with which it is surrounded." "Why, I think it the greatest of wonders."

Reader, my time was a dead loss while I was in file, going up and down that passage to see that image. I would not turn round in my shoes to look at it again.

On entering the art building, I will not pen any thoughts—that fill my soul to overflowing. After a time I moved a few yards to the right, where the Cain and Abel statuary stood. The little fellows, about two feet high, beautiful—so beautiful to the mother who loves little boys—the left arm resting on each waist. Abel's countenance full of frank, loving spirit; had not so many been around I should have kissed Abel. Cain equally handsome, but close examined, there was an unmistakable expression in the eye and lip—with his right arm drawn back, his little fist clinched tight, ready to hit the fatal rap. Thus Cain, hugged with his left arm, and ready to kiss his brother, while the right arm was executing his murderous design. That is just the treatment I have received from citizens in my native place. They have not murdered me, but done far worse. That building, and mostly every building upon the ground, was explored by my searching eye. And, reader, come and talk with me, and see how long I can talk of this, that and all things generally on the Centennial grounds, also to and from the passage from my own cottage home.

On returning from the Centennial, there was, on the seat in front of me, a young man from 20 to 25 years old, whom the conductor found to be on the wrong train. The young man appeared to be honest and unaccustomed to travel. Some talk ensued, the conductor demanded his fare, and the young man handed him a five dollar bill to take it from. When the conductor gave back the change, I said to the young man, " that conductor would have drawn out leviathan with a hook, before he would that money from me." Some cautious advice I gave him, for I had seen new needs all the time of my absence.

In the winter William Bacheller leaves the High School, and applies to me for instruction. In December 27th, 28th, and 29th, I attended State Teachers' Institute, Springfield, (of which I am a member), having a week's vacation. Willie recited till April 1st, 1877, taking in that time eighty lessons, not losing a day or changing the hour except vacation—Christmas week. In that time he mastered physiology, having 40 or 50 lessons; writing compositions by topics on each lesson. Commencing Greenleaf's General Arithmetic at Percentage, completing the book.

In Anderson's Ancient History, he repeated to fourteenth century, in Mediæval, and through Single Entry in Fulton & Eastman's Book-keeping.

Willie is thus enabled to be of great service to his father in business capacity, having been thoroughly and practically drilled. And my eye will follow the boy now, eighteen years of age, till time is no more with us on earth.

December 27th, 1876.—My fiftieth birthday I was at State Teachers' Institute at Springfield, reaching said place about noon on Whitney's train, Whitney taking my ticket just past Indian Orchard. Putting my purse in my overskirt pocket when we reached Springfield, as I rose to leave the car, taking hold of said pocket going along, I stopped. *My pocket-book is not in my pocket!* Man : " You could not have dropped it, madam.") My pocket-book is here within three feet. raising my arm across the aisle. Man : " Let the passengers get out and you will find it, *if dropped.*" "*The passengers, sir, can wait till my pocket-book is forthcoming.*" (A smile pervaded the *frail sex* at my imperativeness.) *The man* was dressed like a gentleman. Man got down on all fours under the seat, and soon came forth; " You did drop it, madam." That man had the inside seat with me in the car, a perfect stranger, and he had picked my pocket. My resolute decision alone found my pocket-book. And there has been a continuation of the same disposition manifested in different ways toward me as if to filch me of my last dollar in my old age!

April Term, 1877.—Mr. Kittredge's railroad case to be tried, the jury upon the ground ten minutes more or less, and have a jolly time the remaining time in the "big shop" here and there. The lawyers effect a settlement, and the "big shop" rings. Kittredge gets $50 after paying costs, &c. Readers, I have been told the settlement was to be told to be, as the assessment. The railroad defendants—*fresh* courage take in their success in that mode of settlement— demanded Mr. Tyler's railroad case to be tried this term The conduct of the jurymen on the Kittredge case—as report has it, their expression and language over its great appraisal—was heralded over town, and round about, the other two would have the same fate. Mr. Tyler's case was not tried. Report has it (and true) said church directors and church advisors prayerfully entreated Mr. D. Whiting making further strides in offers made by *special parties*, without avail.

Town meeting, April, 1877.—Time changed by new by-law from March to April; and the proceedings in seven by nine room caucuses were many and contentious, as report had it. The railroad men were going to oust Dr. Tyler any-how, beginning these notable gatherings with the watchword "New officers, clean ticket," &c., &c. New board of selectmen and assessors; the caucuses were in such a wrangle. DeBevoise comes to the rescue by preaching the Sabbath previous to the above day, to the great disgust of many of his hearers. Condensed it is this : "Let well enough alone," in tone, &c., "you have got to do as I say." DeBevoise's spirit and the consequence of his preaching was manifest on Monday, and this same spirit of his in a more ferocious degree manifesting itself on a future Monday in this book named "The Bears" (not of Wall street,) but North Brookfield, Mass., after prayer—not by DeBevoise—began their work in good earnest. Chairman Bates—Now they are started with a rush, like as "aforetime." The readers can imagine said meeting, which was amusing as well as disgusting to me. Soon DeBevoise comes, with good deal of *vim* apparent; seats near my side. I just bow; no notice! I will here say that I did not enter my railroad case until the December term of the court, 1876, waiting till within a few hours of time when the year would be ended, since the decision of the County Commissioner's award was announced on record at court, December 2d, 1875. During that year I assiduously made every effort to have my land damage claim adjudicated, the defendants well understanding the amount that would be required to liquidate the same; but not an offer but the commissioners, or rather their own assessment, always adding, "you will not have anything to show if you go to law." Some of the most rabid would say to me: "We shall keep you in the court till all you have got is spent; what lawyer will you employ then?" &c.

Thus I have been goaded many times by church members more than by those not within "that vail." The first time I met DeBevoise after the railroad directors' notification of the above suit pending, he did not see me; other times he would evade me by circuiting; in fact it is my best judgment he has not so much as bowed his head when unavoidably meeting me a dozen times since January, 1877, though meeting me fifty times more or less. It took me long, ere I could allege to him his weakness, so often promulgated by others, and when obliged too, I thus announced—DeBe. has catered to his surroundings till he is emasculated of common sense! The old board of selectmen was re-elected, and a new board of assessors—it was a warfaring day. The meeting was adjourned one week to finish town business. Bates took it upon himself to have a new sexton to the town hall. On entering the hall, this second town meeting, by the bell rope stood Bates hugging John Hebard. (Reader, the reason of this last character being brought in is he figures in the cell during my incarceration there.) I stepped out to Duncan and Delvey. and told Delvey the above sight. Delvey replied, "Bates has got an axe to grind." Yes, and it's to prevent my coming to earn my daily papers. As one of Bates' expressions had been, "we must shut Miss Hill's wind all off." And thus every railroad man in town has plied his influence. At this meeting school-room was demanded, and Dr. Tyler said he had been looking at a pleasant large room, with recitation room, in Stone Block (said block was built with the railroad, thus aiding the builders from $500 to $1,000, in being furnished with stone from the Stoddard and King quarry to build up an immense fill for said building, grading the road, etc., improved the looks and prospects of dwelling-stands thousands of dollars); said room was rented for the purpose at once. DeBe. being one of the school committee though he had announced in every examination he should not remain on the committee, for reasons, etc., another year. DeBe. being a supply at that time through resignation of his predecessor. At this town meeting somebody was like to be elected that had not been railroad, etc. DeBe. breaks right in and gets his name re-elected without one word of scruple apparent. Thus DeBe. is school committee for '77. In the Post Office I met DeBe., and said to him, "Mr. DeBevoise I wish you to consider me an applicant to teach the school in Stone Block. You, sir, know well my qualifications,"—De-Be. going from me while speaking—"you will thus inform the other committee." De Be.: "Yes 'm." The week had not ended before I was informed John Hebard was going to stop my coming into that hall, he be d—d if he would seat me (well knowing there would never be a chance). I'll kick up something that will land her to the bottom of the stairs." I was in the hall a few times while he was janitor, but availing myself of other escort. Said Hebard, from truthful reports, is not trustworthy, and thus held by honorable citizens. In due time De B. resigns, and is succeeded by the Rev. Mr. Avann, (Methodist). See the card play.

June 25th, 1877.—Not one offer to purchase my grass. The prospects of a medium crop appeared good, Therefore Patrick O'Brien and Robert Morse were hired by me to harvest, &c., my grass. Mrs. Wm. H. Ayres, in whose employ is Robert Morse (colored), rented me her large heavy span of horses, mowing machine, cart, and tools generally, my haying going on with rapidity. I will say here, father used to cut this two-acre lot first, my grass being early; therefore if the hay was to be made under my supervision, it must be in season for so doing; I after cut over a ton of first quality of rowen.

I also employed Thomas Ashby and his son Fred. to take up half of scaffold floor, and use the same in framing a partition below, thus adding "bay" to my whole scaffold, giving me ample storage room for seven or eight tons of hay. "My hay being cut, &c., by the best team in the town, current report;" and it was a true one. My haying was first of all, complete in barn, June 30th, having saved four tons and more of best quality and make. While the men were at work, I carried them fresh cold prepared drink and lunch A. M. and P. M., not forgetting. Also directed in all which, and how, by the men asking me, raking after cart as politely as *croquet moves*, rushing seventy-five hay covers (from Mr. Haston) when a shower appeared, to protect the food for dumb beasts, putting most all on, without assistance upon bundles of hay, sixty-five in number, with thunder and lightning, and ere the pins were all fastened, I was drenched more thoroughly than by immersion. Reader, I am a *terrible* sufferer from rheumatism, and am affected the worst in *hot weather*. And since my physical constitution was completely wrecked by the ball club blow, the least extra exercise will throw me into dripping perspiration, obliging me, for my own nervous endurance, to change my apparel three or four times per day, if not a dozen of times, and at the same time using crash towel with salt, wormwood regulator or hot drops, taking regulator at said times which is hot drops, and more so, having other ingredients, making it a great medicinal for me in staving off rheumatism.

Paying O'Brien $2.75 per day, and dinners, &c., Morse $2 per day, &c.

Span, &c., $5 per day, and had I been as wise the summer of 1876, I could have $50 income clear, instead of Sherman's nothing.

July 6th, 1877.—Whiting and Stoddard's case was tried before a sheriff's jury in July; the hearing occupied five days more or less. I was present two days, long enough to see the spirit of the parties concerned. Mr. De Bevoise was present all the time I was there, and report said all through the five days, and the anxiety depicted on his countenance, and his coming forward as if to put words in their mouths, awhile he was, with right hand upon Mrs. Bartlett's or Miss Stoddard's chair; at last he detected with his scrutinizing eye, as he calls it, a spider. DeBevoise: "Mrs. Bartlett, there is a spider in your shawl, I'm afraid it will bite you." That little insect in the shawl's folds *was* not larger than a fly speck. I had to move for the performance. DeBevoise could not fail to understand the expression of my face. And such testimony as was given under oath by church members, and railroad benefited men was enough to fill one with disgust and horror to see how cheap their souls were being weighed. I left. Went to Montpelier to attend the American Institute of Instruction, and every hour was teeming with new avenues of thought; the citizens, so magnanimous, were doubly munificent, going, as I did, from that carnivorous scene. Judge Aldrich, Secretary Dickenson, late principal of the Normal school, Westfield; Professor Walton and many others I am accustomed to meet at those educational meetings—no one from North Brookfield but me. Such scenes are not as attractive as the ball rooms for the class employed, and it is my opinion not one teacher is a member of it.

July 6th and 7th, Stoddard Court.—Tim Clark, merchant, cheap freight recipient, occupied, as report has it, a whole day in Sheriff's Court, costing $100, trying to save railroad defendants. Report had it court expenses were $200 per day. Thus it is apparent that the town railroad defendants must have expended in law in railroad suits nearer $1,500 than $1,000. I think a town meeting ought to be called, and a legal vote taken as to how much money shall the town raise to pay for railroad law suits pending before another suit is tried; because Bates, &c., have repeatedly said that they should keep Miss Hill in court till she would not have a cent left. My advice to these railroad lunatics is, hadn't you better consider the statutes awhile; peradventure Mrs. Hill may find even in Massachusetts counsel, that Bates masons, "big shop" Bacheller, cannot bribe, therefore statutes may be vindicated.

July 10th, 11th, 12th, at Montpelier Institute.—The 12th, 4 o'clock P. M., I leave the lecture hall, as all were requested thus to do who had heard Prof. Marshall and seen his calcium Yosemite views, that the hundreds of citizens might have a chance to enter the hall and thus be recipients of some benefit to be cherished in their memories while they had given so generously and munificently of their rich heritage for the comfort of hundreds of teachers and professors. I wish to mention the Capitol building, though I had read descriptions thereof, the stately grandeur of which was never realized in the least until I mounted those stone steps, and entering, going through the different historical rooms. In the Senate Chamber and Representative Hall, being chosen speaker, I was seated in the judge's chair in both departments, my decision adjourning the court in both

"Houses." We then mounted the tower; being so dizzy, a gentleman escort had to hold me with considerable aid when in the highest audience room "viewing the prospect o'er." To look down around I was too giddy to see but very little, but in the nigh distance those mountain tops round about, those hills and vales, and all upon them so plain to be seen by my naked eye, I was held long speechless in silent adoration to Almighty God. My guide and staff spoke: "You seem dumb." "Yes; the glories to behold." I cannot look down, oh, so sick, but when I raise my eyes up, off, around in the distance all is clear as noon day. It interprets thus: Leave those things about you, get to those beyond and above. I regret I cannot recall the names of my guide and benefactor and wife and the three teachers near-by (my book for names I have not here).

In going down we come to the British relic all readers know about. And there was a learned gentleman with his half dozen lady teachers, all young, flirty, very intelligent you must know. The gentleman had asked each one to examine that relic and tell what a certain mark meant. Not one of those normal graduates had the remotest idea. The gentleman seeing me, says, "Madam, you come here; just stand back; let this lady see; call over the different parts of this relic." The first announced, British private mark. There the old teacher informs first word. Oh, so little thinking is done by students! I mean practical thought.

In the law library and the other. It seemed as if I could stay and learn years, and not be weary. I had bought tickets to Mount Washington, paying $8.75 by way of Wells River—going to the summit from Montpelier, returning through Bethlehem, Littleton, Franconia Notch to Wells River, thence to Worcester; the round trip from Worcester to Montpelier was $8. $16.75 was railroad fares, and $30 less 25 cents, paid every expense; 7 days. Thus young students travel to learn, and be more in God's image. Professor Richards, wife, and sister, Professor Comin of Worcester, and others, took the 5 o'clock train for White Mountains with me. I bought and paid for the first excursion ticket to Mount Washington, the agent sold. Three or four teachers saying, "Why wait till you know who is going, etc. We are to start at 5 P.M., and I am going if the cars can, or will carry me by this ticket." Agent, "I give you a note of introduction to the proprietor of Fabyan House, and your room will be all you can ask or desire." But a happier crew never was in a car room, and in ascending to the top of Mount Washington, 6,000 feet, I was not dizzy once. My eyes stopped not for frivolity, but was taking in knowledge, every fleeting moment, to feed my soul to all eternity. The Crawford Notch, the Bethlehem House, Franconia Notch, the Cascades and Boulder, the Flume House, the Old Man of the Mountain, Echo Lake, the thunder shower at my feet, the Cannon Mountain, Mount Lafayette, the basin, the pool—each speaks volumes to me for meditation. When sitting upon the beam above that huge boulder in Franconia Notch, and the waters rushing on madly, far, far below me, I cried out, "Wilt thou not, Almighty God, reveal to me this wondrous mystery, this work of thine almighty power, that fills me with awe, almost with terror; yet adoration rises; how great and mighty are thy works!!! What is man, that thou art mindful of him?" I returned to hotel, thus walking fourteen miles between 9 A.M. and 4 P.M. I had no infirmity in that mountain air.

In North Brookfield, July 31st, 1877, by Rev. G. H. DeBevoise, Charles A. French and Marion M. Smith, both of this town. Notwithstanding C. A. F. treated his companions in "big shop," according to its requirements, he was serenaded August 1st, at 9:30 P. M. In other words, the very vaults of heaven rung with the hideous noise of the mob, who, with groans, yells, tin pans and horns, boilers, brass kettles, all belched forth, as if in interpretation to be understood by all—this is our vernacular—in open violation of the revised by-laws of the town, under article fourth, sections first and seventh. Mr. and Mrs. French, seniors, being in a very feeble state of health; Mr. French lying at the point of death many days, and his life despaired of for weeks, was just able to get around. His wife was in a recent paralyzing condition, making them both suffer intensely from the savage noise, and insult. Charles, seeing his father's and mother's mental suffering, was tempted almost to use his gun, Charley's report has it saw Bothwell and Foster. At any rate, I saw the Furnace boy in its scene, a boisterous, actor ; and I saw a man in the distance I called Bothwell. Said men, if it was them—and I am very sure it was—did not arrest any of the party and put them in the felon's cell, but let them bellow a long time, and then said "dry up" though their savage noise was heard miles, and the kettles, trucks, of all descriptions, left about said French's yard, etc. I was leaving Alden Olmstead's house, as some of the actors passed me, and took pains to spot that proceeding, being reporter, you will remember.

So much for officers and by-laws. It was spoken of as a "rich thing" by many citizens.

August 17th, 1877.—The North Brookfield little semi-monthly journal issued the following : "A few days since we had the pleasure of conversing with a gentleman on this subject, hearing a laughable account of his observations in a neighboring town that is out of debt. He said there had been five suicides within two years. There was no public or private enterprise, a strawshop had been in operation but the proprietor had moved the stock to an adjoining town that had a debt and offering the buildings at ruinous prices. There were a few young men, nearly all moving out of town when they became of age, and those that remained were idiots. It all goes to show that if a town wishes any public improvement it must have money, and this makes debt, &c." Reader, I was astonished that the editor had not common sense enough to know the above mentioned gentleman was ridiculing North Brookfield, Mass. Five suicides have taken place within the two years in said North Brookfield, two of them being so near the "big shop" had it not been for obstacles between, the blood and brains of the two men might have sprinkled posts at two meeting houses, Methodist, and First Congregational Church, but those marvelously con-structed brains. Had there been no obstacles, which were bespattered with brains, and blood, and said blood &c., had reached the posts thereof they would have called it a "biblical symbol pass-over," I believe.

As for the young men above mentioned (I ought to know) I will say this "It is putty much so." As for the straw-shop—I don't know, but am informed on reliable authority—that incident belongs to our midst also.

Said journal also states if the Southbridge and Brookfield Railroad makes its terminus at East Brookfield—and it is probable it will be—it will be largely due to the untiring efforts of T. C. Bates who has given and is still devoting much time and attention to the work. Selah. Free rides loom prospectively in the late glassware drummer's mind. How many dollars I shall have saved on car fares, say nothing more, I shall soon be railroad king," &c.

August, 1877.—I have decided to build me a large room 15 feet by 17 to join my barn and wood-house, giving me recitation room and entrance into barn, which I have for years been saving of my small income to do. Thirty years to-day I laid my beautiful babe (my second born) in the cold, silent tomb. Thus my monument for my four lost boys and L. shall be completed together. My wall must be built this fall round the railroad, to shield me from those engine spark fires. Oh! how much expense that railroad has been to me. $300 will not draw the stone and build the wall. See the devastation of my property to make a dozen or more *wealthy*. And the treatment I have received from those men, the illegality of their proceedings in open defiance of the statutes, makes them as eligible to State prison as the Northampton bank robbers, and more so ; they are robbing the widows and fatherless. And my every effort which has been untiring has been contemptuously maltreated. In the words of old Legree in Uncle Tom's Cabin, "D—n you, we've got you ; help yourself if you can." Thus I am hampered by those ravenous wolves for money. I will start this minute and tell Alden Bacheller, who is being made from poor to rich by this road, he must without delay remove the posts of railroad fence upon my land, for I shall build a wall in September to protect my mowings. At his store I said : "Mr. Bacheller, don't notice nor even look at me.

I mean business, and at once." "Mrs. Hill, I have heard enough about that; the railroad fence will not be meddled with, and I don't want to hear anything more about it. The posts on my land will be ousted if you don't remove them. I suppose an action for trespass can be issued. I wish the assistance you give the lawyers." "But now hear, Bacheller, I never will speak to you about this or that on railroad adjustment with me again. The defendants will have to apply to me, or meet the law." Bacheller: "I guess we can stand the law as long as you can," etc. *Exit.*

I then made my way to Mrs. Wm. H. Ayres to hire R. Morse to cut my rowen. The rowen is cut and dried without being wet, Mr. Haston and Mahoney assisting. They say there is over a ton of it. It looks so good, I almost think I might eat with "Nebuchadnezzar." Robert is hired till my work is completed, more or less, when Mrs. Ayres does not want him at her work. At Worcester, to buy windows, doors and shingles, for building my L, at Forbush & Co., trade made cash on delivery, the time September, to be completed. I have my $50 bank book, money invested when working for Barnard, and Sumner & Co., in 1861 or '62. I go to bank for said investment (Mrs. Wm. H. Beecher having said book in her custody till within a few weeks of her death in 1870), Mrs. Beecher causing it to be thus kept so that I might have an income accumulating. The clerk takes the book, saying, "We have paid you your interest." Very true; upon another investment. Impudently—"How came you by two books?" "By asking an eminent lawyer you know well, and his investing where he thought best, I directing him thus to do. I did not know what bank till said lawyer gave me the book." "We never give out two books." "Sir, I have two," &c. My bank book is still there, but a young lawyer was called to protect the same from the bank thieves, and a law suit is to come of that, and, reader, I will state publicly how it ends, by the press. I then go on to G. H. Clark's store and get a witness, and give the other book in presence of the witness for $450. I was not quite ready to have that taken too. My aged counsel tells me I must be ready for court in September. I demur.

He asked me if I had counsel ready to meet my case, "for I tell you, Mrs. Hill, I do nothing in court." "My case cannot be tried, as my most important witness is not in the United States, and cannot be. Squire: "I tell you, Mrs. Hill, *you must be ready*. The town will not let it be *put* over. I think, sir, I know too well about court. At the time of Duncan's Court I plead with tears, being the plaintiff, to have the hearing in September and December, and was obliged to wait till last of March; Judge Aldrich calming me by saying I must wait till December. Squire: "The town is ready, and want it settled—and I, the injured party, won't pay for that town's depredations and robbery. Not much of a look, when counsel pleads for town instead of party employing him. The town will be informed who my counsel is the day of the sitting of said court. They will then have ample time to make tenders. In full bubble I pass into the street, starting for Court House; when about half way there I met the legal adviser of the town. " You will please, sir, not think, or make effort to have my railroad suit (entered December last) have a hearing this coming court. I am not ready, and cannot be for good reason ; and sir, I trust you as a gentleman, that no attempt will be made by the town, who have my property stolen in possession, thus making costs. "Mrs. Hill, you will have no trouble," &c. " Thanks." I then went to the other counsel; he being absent, I left word my case could not be heard, and should said V. make an effort for his thief clients it will be as though he was talking to the " old man in the mountain." He (V.) will remember my effort to have Duncan's trial hastened. "You anything more to offer?" "No, sir—good day." I then told my brother's counsel I had in possession papers beneficial to his case, and I wish it could have been otherwise. My case first, as I have the papers and much better prepared for this issue. Brother's counsel : " I shan't try it." "Has any one asked you to ?" I have not had, neither wished for any legal advice on my railroad case since the appointment of railroad bonds. I have full knowledge of the statute's requirements. I then said, " I wish you, gentlemen, to bring my brother's case to a successful issue." Counsel for brother: "Tyler must come down so and so." I " can't see what you wish him to come down for, &c. He cannot add a word, nor wish to take from, as he well knows I have every point at issue, is well prepared, which will be irrevocable, conclusive evidence in the power of faithful counsel to bring judgment in his favor, &c." Notwithstanding all that!!! my brother was summoned next day to come at once to prepare for court. Reader, I trust you have checked. My brother *went down, and down it was.* And the appalling expense of court and demand for so much money, &c. The next morning, at an early hour my brother was waited on by deputized agent *for first time* since the commissioners' award, and the settlement was effected in part, and concluded finally next day, to my astonishment. But I availed myself of being down to court Monday. Judge Aldrich presiding, saw and heard the jury sworn. My brother's counsel coming to me and asking for said brother, I said " He has complied with your directions." " Why did not he send me word?" &c. " You could not expect me to come to your office after heralding; you told me you would enter my case, and that's all, &c. You have not entered my case, nor put it over. I effected my case— not being on this term court—with the town's counsel, my only expense for the term, is its fee, I trust; I can ill afford this bleeding.

This is 3d September, 1877.

COMMONWEALTH OF MASSACHUSETTS, } ss.:
  Worcester,

At a meeting of the County Commissioners begun and holden at Worcester, within and for the County of Worcester, on the second Tuesday of September, A. D. 1875, and by adjournment on the first day of December, A. D. 1875.

To the Honorable, the County Commissioners, within and
  for the County of Worcester:

Respectfully represents your petitioner Elizabeth R. Hill, of North Brookfield, in said county, that she has been for a long time and now is, the owner of two certain tracts of land situated in said North Brookfield. First tract of about six acres bounded south by a highway running by the Walnut Grove Cemetery, east by said cemetery, north by road leading from North Brookfield to East Brookfield, west by road leading from Moses Tyler's to Spunky Hollow, so called.

Second tract bounded on the east by said last named road, south by land of Mrs. A. B. Stoddard, west by said Stoddard's land, north by road from North to East Brookfield, and containing about two acres; said tracts are only separated by said Spunky Hollow Road.

That the North Brookfield Railroad Company, a railroad corporation duly organized, have laid out and located their railroad while your petitioner was the owner of said tracts, through both of said tracts, running easterly and westerly through the same, taking a strip five rods wide through each of said tracts, and have taken about .804 acres from the first above described lot and about .350 acres from the second described tract, as per plan furnished your petitioner by said railroad company, thereby causing great damage to your petitioner, separating said tracts into four tracts, and leaving what they do not take in bad and inconvenient shape and otherwise greatly injuring those portions of said tracts not taken, and have taken and converted to their own use large quantities of stone wall standing on said tract; and your petitioner was obliged to cut a large number of valuable trees standing and growing upon said tracts; and have discontinued said Spunky Hollow road by filling up the same and obstructing the travel thereon; and your petitioner is unable to agree with said company as to her damages.

Wherefore your petitioner prays that your Honorable Board, after due notice to all persons interested, will view the premises and assess your petitioner said damages in the premises, and order all such culverts, cattle guards, crossings and structures as are necessary and proper, to be made by said railroad company, and also pray the said railroad company may be required by your Honorable Board to give satisfactory security to your petitioner for any damages and costs that may be assessed by your Board or a jury.

North Brookfield, Mass., Sept. 3d, 1875.

ELIZABETH R. HILL.

COMMONWEALTH OF MASSACHUSETTS, } ss. :
Worcester,

At a meeting of the County commissioners begun and holden at Worcester, within and for the County of Worcester, on the third Tuesday of June, A. D. 1875, and by adjournment on the third day of September, A. D. 1875.

On the petition aforesaid it is ordered, that the petitioner notify the said North Brookfield Railroad Company, that said County Commissioners will meet at the Town Hall in said North Brookfield, in said County, on Friday the fifteenth day of October, at ten of the clock in the forenoon, by serving said railroad company with an attested copy of said petition and this order fourteen days at least before the time of said meeting, that they may then and there appear and show cause why the prayer of said petition should not be granted.

BOND.

KNOW ALL MEN BY THESE PRESENTS, That the North Brookfield Railroad Company, by Bonum Nye, President of said Railroad Company, duly authorized by a vote of the Board of Directors passed Dec. 31, 1875, as principal, and Alden Batcheller, William H. Montague, John B. Dewing, of said North Brookfield, as sureties, are holden and stand firmly bound and obliged unto Elizabeth R. Hill, of said North Brookfield, in the full and just sum of three thousand dollars, to be paid unto the said Elizabeth R. Hill, her executors, administrators or assigns; to the which payment, well and truly to be made, we bind ourselves and our heirs, executors and administrators, firmly by these presents.

Witness our hands and seals, dated the thirty-first day of December, in the year of our Lord one thousand eight hundred and seventy-five.

The condition of this obligation is such, That whereas the said North Brookfield Railroad Company have located their railroad in said North Brookfield on land of said Elizabeth R. Hill, and taken the same for the construction of the said railroad, and thereby causing damage to her; now, therefore, if the said railroad company shall well and truly pay the said Elizabeth R. Hill the amount of damages and costs she may be legally entitled to, as may be assessed by the county commissioners or a jury, then this bond is null and void, otherwise to remain in full force and virtue.

North Brookfield Railroad Company by
Bonum Nye, Pres. [L. S.]
By vote of Board of Directors,

In presence of   Alden Batcheller, [L. S.]
Charles Duncan,   W. H. Montague, [L. S.]
E. D. Batcheller.   John B. Dewing. [L. S.]

[No. 346.]

Worcester, ss.

Clerk's Office of the County Commissioners.

Costs taxed by order of said Commissioners on the petition of Elizabeth R. Hill, for assessment of damages, *vs.* North Brookfield R. R. Co.:

Services of Commissioners........................$15 00
Report for Record......... ....
Examining Road for Acceptance ....
Printer's Bill.....................................
Officer's Fees....................................
Clerk's Fees—
    Entry, &c......................... $1 25
    Order of Notice................... 1 60
    Clerk's term fees for two terms, at 40 cents a term..................... 80
    Record.... .... 1 00
    Copy of Report................... 1 60
                                         6 25
                                            $21 25

Worcester, ———, 18

Received of ——— ———, the sum of ——— dollars and ——— cents, in full for the above costs.

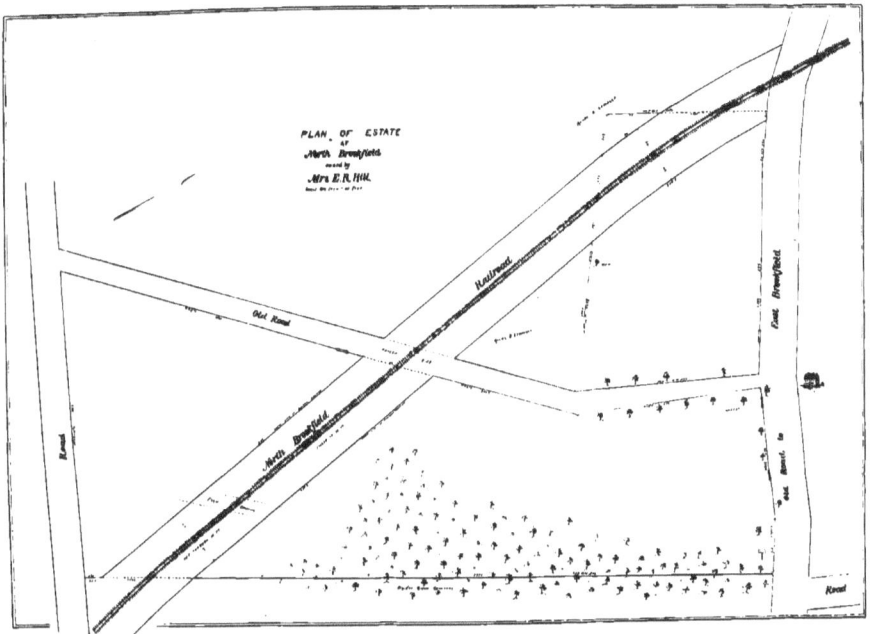

WARRANT FOR TOWN MEETING.

Worcester, ss.:

To SYLVANDER BOTHWELL, Constable of the Town of North Brookfield, in said County,

Greeting:

In the name of the Commonwealth of Massachusetts, you are directed to notify the inhabitants of the town of North Brookfield, qualified to vote in elections, and town officers, to meet at the Town Hall, in said North Brookfield, on Friday, the 29th day of January, inst., at ten of the clock A. M., there and then to act on the following articles:

1st. To choose a Moderator, to preside in said meeting.

2d. To see if the town will vote to subscribe for and hold shares in the capital stock of the North Brookfield Railroad Company, a railroad corporation, to be formed under chapter 53 of the Acts of the year 1872, for the purpose of building a railroad from North Brookfield to East Brookfield.

3d. To see if the town will vote to become an associate for the formation of the North Brookfield Railroad Company, a railroad corporation to be formed under chapter 53 of the Acts of the year 1872, for the purpose of building a railroad from North Brookfield to East Brookfield.

4th. To see what action the town will take in regard to raising money to aid in building a railroad from North Brookfield to East Brookfield, and act thereon.

And you are directed to serve this warrant, by posting up attested copies thereof; one at the Town House, and one at the Post Office, in said town, seven days at least, before the time of holding said meeting.

Thereof fail not to make due return of this warrant, with your doings thereon, to the Town Clerk, at the time and place of meeting aforesaid.

Given under our hands this 22d day of January, in the year 1875.

WARREN TYLER,   } Selectmen
GEO. C. LINCOLN,   } of
JOHN B. DEWING, } North Brookfield.

(A true copy.)

Attest—SYLVANDER BOTHWELL, }
    Constable of North Brookfield.

LEASE OF THE NORTH BROOKFIELD RAILROAD

TO THE

BOSTON & ALBANY RAILROAD COMPANY.

This Indenture,

Made this first day of January, A. D. 1876, by and between the North Brookfield Railroad Company, a corporation created by the Commonwealth of Massachusetts, party of the first part; and the Boston & Albany Railroad Company, a corporation created by said Commonwealth, with whose road the road of said party of the first part connects in the Town of Brookfield, in said commonwealth, party of the second part,

Witnesseth, That the said party of the first part doth hereby grant, lease, demise and let unto the said party of the second part, its successors and assigns, the North Brookfield Railroad, that is to say, the whole of the railroad of said party of the first part, extending from the depot building on the line of the Boston & Albany Railroad at East Brookfield Village, in the Town of Brookfield, Massachusetts, to and into the town of North Brookfield, Massachusetts, as far as the village, and to the line of the shoe factory of Messrs. E. & A. H. Batchellor & Company, with all the real estate, rights, powers, easements, tenements, franchises, privileges and appurtenances and equipment appurtenant to said railroad, or belonging to said North Brookfield Railroad Company, and all the branch tracks, turnouts, depot grounds, stations, both freight and passenger buildings, car houses, engine houses, water tanks and water rights, turntables, superstructure and fixtures connected, or used with, or belonging to said railroad, or to said North Brookfield Railroad Company, and all lands upon which the same are now situated, or which belong to or have been taken by said company, whether included in its location or not, and wherever situated; and all personal property connected or designed for use, with all or any part of the premises hereby demised; except the hall in the second story of the brick depot over the passenger rooms, which hall said party of the first part shall have the right to rent or use, but for such purposes only as shall not be injurious to the interests of said party of the second part.

To have and to hold the said railroad and other premises hereby demised unto the said Boston & Albany Railroad Company, its successors and assigns, for and during the full term of ten years from the first day of January, A. D. 1876. And said party of the first part agree that said Boston & Albany Railroad Company shall have the sole and exclusive right, during said term, to hold, use and enjoy, run and operate the premises hereby demised; to fix, establish, collect, receive and retain for its own use and benefit all tolls, fares, rents, or compensation for the use thereof or for any transportation, or for anything done therewith or thereon, except as hereby otherwise provided, and at its expense and pleasure to use or authorize any one to use the name of said party of the first part, whenever necessary or convenient to enforce, secure, retain or enjoy any right or thing hereby granted, demised, promised or given, and any such authority to revoke.

Said party of the first part agrees, at its own expense, during said term to execute all instruments and to do all things required by law or reasonably requested by the said party of the second part; to preserve and maintain the corporate rights and existence of said party of the first part and its legal organization from year to year and at all times, or which may be necessary or reasonably requested by said party of the second part to confirm, secure, protect, and assure to said party of the second part all and whatever is hereby granted, demised, promised or given to said party of the second part; and to do all things which said party of the first part is required by law to do, except those which said party of the second part hereby agrees or is hereby permitted to do.

And the said party of the first part agrees to assume and pay all taxes, whether National, State County, Town, or other taxes that shall in any way be directly or indirectly either legally assessed upon or to said party of the first part, or upon or to its property, road, franchises, business, receipts or income, whether assessed to or against the said party of the first part or said party of the second part, or shall be assessed upon the capital stock of said party of the first part to either of the parties hereto.

The said party of the second part, in consideration of the above premises, covenants and agrees with the said party of the first part, that it, the said party of the second part will, with its own servants and rolling stock, and at its own expense, run and operate said North Brookfield Railroad hereby demised, excepting always that portion of said railroad which extends from the depot of said party of the first part, in the Town of North Brookfield, to the stop of Messrs. E. & A. H. Batcheller & Company, during the term of this lease, in such a manner as shall be reasonable and proper for a railroad of its class and description and for the business upon its route, running such trains as may be found necessary for the reasonable accommodation of the public. But said party of the first part agrees that said party of the second part may either permit any one or more persons or corporations at any time or times, or from time to time, both to do or cause to be done, all transportation which shall be done, or which any one shall be entitled to have done upon or over said above excepted portion of said railroad, and to use and occupy said portion, and also all such part or parts of any property or premises hereby demised as lie or lies west of said depot in North Brookfield, or may itself use, occupy and operate said portion, part or parts in any way.

Said party of the second part hereby covenants and agrees during said term of ten years, at its own expense, to keep all the property and premises hereby demised, excepting the said above excepted portion of said railroad, and such portion, part or parts of said property and premises as said party of the first part hereby agrees that said party of the second part may permit any other persons or corporations to use and occupy, in as good condition, and to keep said excepted portion, part or parts, in as safe condition, reasonable wear and tear in each case excepted, as the same respectively were in, when received by and delivered to said party of the second part, and also to pay any and all damages for which said party of the first part shall in any way become liable for loss of, or injury to life, limb, persons or property, incurred by or in either the running or use of said railroad, or of any part of the premises hereby demised by any person or corporation, or by or through any act, neglect or omissions of said property of the second part.

The party of the second part hereby covenants and agrees to keep at all times during said term full, just and true accounts of all the gross receipts by it derived from the running of said North Brookfield Railroad, or the use of any property hereby demised, and to make a full report to said party of the first part of said gross receipts semi-annually, that is to say, on the first day of August in each year during said term, for the six months ending with the then next preceding month of June, and on the first day of February, in each year during said term for the six months ending with the then next preceding month of December, and to pay to said party of the first part as rent, and in full compensation for the use of the premises hereby demised annually on the first day of February in each year, during said term, twenty-five per cent., of what shall remain of the entire gross receipts aforesaid, for the year ending with the month of December, then next preceding, after deducting from said gross receipts, before any appropriation or payment of any part thereof, for any other purpose, the sum of two thousand dollars ($2,000), which sum shall be retained by said party of the second part, for its own use and benefit as compensation for the use by it on said North Brookfield Railroad of the rolling stock of said party of the second part, for that year.

And it is further stipulated and agreed by and between the parties hereto, that the price of one first class passenger's fare from North Brookfield village to East Brookfield, or from East Brookfield to North Brookfield village shall not exceed fifteen cents per trip, and the rate of freight transportation between said points shall not exceed seventy cents per ton, and for coal in car loads shall not exceed fifty cents per gross ton.

And it is further agreed that said party of the second part shall have the right to make special freight contracts or rates for transportation with heavy shippers at as much less rates as they choose, but in which event the *pro rata* portion of actual receipts shall be credited and allowed as receipts from the North Brookfield Railroad at the same rate per mile on freight and passengers transported over any part of it, and of the Boston & Albany Railroad, as said party of the second part receives on the same.

And it is further agreed by and between the parties hereto that the said party of the second part shall have the right to make, lay and construct any tracks, buildings, additions or alterations and permanent improvements which its directors shall think fit to make to or on said North Brookfield Railroad, its construction, road, tracks, superstructure, depots and appurtenances, or in or on any part or parts of the property or premises hereby demised during said term of ten years, all such tracks, buildings, additions, alterations and improvements, if any to be made at the expense of said party of the second part, and at no cost whatever to said party of the first part, unless it, the said party of the first part shall have been consulted in relation to the same, prior to their being done, and shall have agreed in writing or by a formal vote of its directors to assume or share the expense thereof.

And it is further stipulated and agreed that the party of the first part may at any time build or cause to be built, at its own risk and expense, such building or buildings upon its grounds as it may deem necessary for its business interests, if the party of the second part shall have been first consulted in regard to their location and building and have consented thereto in writing or by a formal vote of the directors.

And it is further agreed and understood that the entire rolling stock and equipment and all other personal property furnished by the party of the second part for the operation or use of all or any part of said North Brookfield Railroad or any purpose, and any real property so furnished, except such buildings and tracks as shall be affixed to the real estate of said North Brookfield Railroad Company, shall remain at all times the property of the said party of the second part, and may be removed or held by it at any time and for its own use and benefit.

And it is further stipulated and agreed that in case any difference shall arise as to the construction or effect of any stipulation herein contained or as to any claim arising under the same, the same shall be submitted to the arbitration of three persons, who shall be mutually agreed upon by the parties hereto, and the award of all or a majority of said three persons shall be final in the premises.

And it is further understood and agreed by each party hereto, that all promises and agreements hereby made by such party are made, and shall be considered to be made with the other party hereto and shall extend to, and enure for the benefit of the successors or assigns of the party with or to whom or for whose benefit such agreement or promises are made.

In witness whereof the said North Brookfield Railroad Company, by Bonum Nye, its president, hereto duly authorized, and the said Boston & Albany Railroad Company, by D. Waldo Lincoln, its vice president, hereto duly authorized, have hereto and to one other instrument of like tenor and date herewith, signed their corporate names, and set their common seals the day and year first above written.

At a meeting of the Board of Directors of the Boston & Albany Railroad Company, duly held in the City of Boston, on the 13th day of February, 1877, an indenture of Lease of the North Brookfield Railroad Company, as above written, was submitted and considered, and it was thereupon

Voted, " That the directors of the Boston & Albany Railroad Company do hereby agree to and approve a lease by the North Brookfield Railroad Company to the Boston & Albany Railroad Company, dated the first day of January, A. D. 1876, for ten years from said first day of January, and all the terms as set forth and contained therein, and that said lease be submitted to the meeting of the stockholders of said Boston & Albany Railroad Company, to be held in Boston on the 14th day of February, current for the purpose of seeing if said stockholders will approve of the same and of said terms.

[Attest,]   J. A. RUMRILL,
Secretary and Clerk of the Boston & Albany R. R. Co.

[*Spencer Sun*, August 3d, 1877.]

THE RAILROAD CASE.

Mr. EDITOR,—The proper appraisal of land taken by towns or corporations for public purposes, is a subject important to all concerned; and a right understanding of the law in relation to it may save much trouble and expensive litigation. All know that such taking is authorized by law, and wisely so, as without such power no public improvement could be made. If the consent of all parties must be obtained, no enterprise, great or small, could be accomplished. The law not only provides for the taking of the land, but secures to the owner the proper facilities for obtaining a fair compensation for the same, and any damage sustained in the premises.

In the first place, by agreement of the parties. If that is not effected, then by appraisal of the county commissioners; and in case their doings should not satisfy, then a sheriff's jury called upon the premises again to consider the question; and if their estimate of the value of the land taken exceeds the amount awarded by the commissioners, the cost in both cases falls on the corporation; or the party may appeal directly from the commissioners to the court.

That jurors and appraisers sometimes adopt a wrong standard of value in such cases, is evidenced by the decision of the case of the heirs of Dexter Stoddard vs. The North Brookfield Railroad Co.

The question in such cases is, not what the land taken is worth to the railroad corporation, neither is the fictitious price that the owner is pleased to place on the property to be considered. Either of these considerations might as effectually block the wheels of any enterprise as if no rights had been secured in that connection.

The decision must be based on the cash value of the land, if sold for any other purpose; and if adjoining lands are damaged in consequence, what compensation should be made for such injury.

It is not a consideration to be urged in such cases that the land is taken without the consent of the owner; that he does not wish to part with it; that he is able to keep it; that it has an especial value on account of its having been inherited from ancestors more or less remote—but simply the market value of the land. That is what the law in the case proposes to secure to the aggrieved party; not his fanciful estimate of value from any other consideration. To illustrate. You are responsible for killing my horse. I set up the claim the horse was a great favorite; that I had owned him long and did not want to part with him; that he was safe for all my family to use—and I claim $150 damage.

The fact of the case is that the horse was not (for sale) worth one third of the amount. What should I name as a compensation, the net market value of the animal, or my constructive estimate? Such an appraisal might injure my feelings, and perhaps be a net loss; but what other standard of value could judicious men adopt in the case? This was the mistake made by the party to this suit, and we think by some of the jurors that sat on the case. Two sets of men, neither of whom had any personal interest to affect their judgment, had considered and decided the amount of damage, and it would seem that the claimant ought to have relied somewhat on their judgment. In addition to this, the railroad directors were extremely anxious to settle all these claims without litigation, and to accomplish this they made offers exceeding their own and the commissioners' valuation. But all to no effect. A sheriff's jury came on; five days were spent on the trial; and, but for the extravagant appraisal of some of the jurors, made under oath, the amount of the award would not exceed that of the county commissioners, and was, in fact, fifty dollars less than the directors had offered, for the sake of a settlement. The other party, whose case would have come before the same jury, very wisely concluded to settle as proposed by the directors.

Thinking that the history of this case might benefit the public, I offer it for publication in your paper.

North Brookfield, July 30. W.

[*Spencer Sun*, August 17, 1877.]

Reply to "W.'s" Letter of Aug. 3d.

The appraisal of land taken by towns or corporations for public purposes authorized by law, etc. Said right needs no argument. But land taken for such purposes should be appraised by disinterested men, as the law directs, previous to taking, except for making surveys, is of great moment, as the "cases" referred to have proven. Then the parties aggrieved would seldom have recourse to courts. Some of the men appointed to assess damage on land taken by the North Brookfield Railroad Company, were objected to in writing before their appraisal of said land, as disqualified, etc., and a request for legal arbiters from the Board of Directors was refused! The North Brookfield Railroad land damage rendered (as the report has it) $15,390.47-100, of which three out of the five appraisers took to themselves of that sum $7,545 for their damage. (Richly, appraisers, gentlemen, swallow that, will you, and call it disinterested.) The changeable judgment of the above referees upon some of the land damage claimants, was as follows : Lewis Whiting case, first assessment, $560, next, $750, next, $800, next, $900, final commissioners, $1,150—thus you see judgment varied $590 worth. Daniel Whiting case, first assessment, $1,050, next, $1,100, next, $1,200, next, $1,300, next, $1,400 —final commissioners, $1,456. Wm. P. Haskell, bakery, for loss of business, he received $1,000. "Said business, he was sick of, and had been trying to sell out for more than six months previous!" W. Dean, butcher, $350 ; F. Stoddard, grocer, $400. The argument of these appraisers was, " they can hold a lawsuit and we must pay them well." A. and E. Batcheller, building a stand, etc., occupied by three men just mentioned. Mr. A. Batcheller had said in one of the rallying. railroad meetings, " if the company would give him $4,000 for his place he should take it, or even $3,000." But the appraisers marched up boldly and gave them $6,000, and the occupants $1,750! Joseph Kimball, $133, for one acre 957-1000, out of a farm valued at $800, for 80 acres, cutting through the most worthless part of it, a mud swamp, draining and filling, etc. If a suitable fence and cattle guards were made, as the statutes require, an improvement to his farm. Freeman Walker's case, $75 for one acre, 240-1000, out of a pasture of nine acres valued $100, and said sum he paid for said pasture a few years previous. The land taken fit only (one would think) as a resting place for owls and woodchucks. Advisory "W's" figures on J. Kimball's land was $300, said land joins said "W." One of the arbiters in making report for North Brookfield Railroad, caused to be printed in most of the papers of the State, "That the town would be against any award being granted to land damage claimants above the figures of the appraisers." It is but justice to the parties concerned that the above accurate facts should have equal publicity, and show cause why some aggrieved land claimant desires what the statutes will give. Had advisory "W" been willing that equity should prevail, he would have resigned when required thus to do. Also these public attempts to prejudice and buttonhole whoever may chance to be called jurors, would not have been found in print. Work commenced in July, 1875, on the North Brookfield Railroad, and the commissioners did not come to appraise or to direct road crossing till Oct. 15th, 1875, and April 28th, 1876. Then that body came and complied with all the violation of the statutes by the North Brookfield Railroad Company. The cattle-guards they authorized to be built in place of the "sham ones," is not done yet. The lane they granted to Lewis Whiting to be made by said corporation was annulled by the directors. The commissioners gave in afterwards! The Whiting case was settled through his church friends; and to their great relief, Bonum Nye had interviewed him many times, offering him $100 out of his own pocket, if he would give him three years to pay it in; four others, $50 each. Mr. Whiting settled; he tells me these sums are not paid, and is unhappy because of his settlement.

·The North Brookfield Railroad fence and cattle-guards are a frail sham, and the corporation were notified by a party aggrieved, in writing, within a year after the taking of the land for railroad purposes, that said fence and guards were not safe protection for cattle, therefore, not accepted, together with the assessment, etc. Had the North Brookfield Railroad been built upon the route laid out by J. Gilman, it would, without doubt, be a connecting link to the north and west part of the State.

As it is built, it must ever remain the North Brookfield Branch Road. The grade is such, that with very little extra freight, the train gets stuck, as the Worcester attorneys can testify. At other times, its despairing puffs and tugs are such as to affect the sensitive ear, and draw heartfelt sympathy for the iron horse.

E. R. HILL.

[*Spencer Sun*, August 24th, 1877.]

REPLY TO "W.'s" LETTER OF 3D INST.—(*Continued.*)

As there remains but two land damage claimants, besides the one in equity, to be adjudicated, a few preliminaries bearing, perhaps, on "W.'s" different threads of argument may not be out of place. The Tyler farm, valued for taxation in 1850, $\frac{7}{8}$ house, 2 barns, 79 acres, $3,600; Jenks' farm, house, barn, 146 acres, $3,000; Daniel Gilbert's land, house, barn, 28 acres, $2,000; Freeman Walker, house, barn, $58\frac{1}{4}$ acres, $3,200; Amasa Walker, 2 houses, barn, shed, 57 acres, $7,000; Lewis Whiting, new house, barn, 22 acres, $1,950; John H. Deland, house, barn, $50\frac{1}{2}$ acres, $800; Bonum Nye, house, barn, shop, 105 acres, $3,150; F. A. Potter, 2 houses, barn, shed, $107\frac{3}{4}$ acres, $3,500, Chas. T. Kendrick, $90\frac{3}{4}$ acres, $8,900; David W. Lane, house, barn, 112 acres, $2,400. In 1868: D. Gilbert, house, barn, 36 acres, $3,800; D. Tyler, $\frac{7}{8}$ house, 1 barn, $47\frac{1}{2}$ acres, $3,000; Lewis Whiting, 22 acres, $2,500; F. A. Potter, 108 acres, $3,500; Chas. T. Kendrick, house, barn, 30 acres, $2,000; Jenks, farm, new house, barn, 146 acres, $3,500. In 1862: Tyler farm, house, barn, 47 acres, $4,200; Daniel Gibert, house, barn, 34 acres, $4,500; Jenks' farm, house, barn, 146 acres, $3,900; Lewis Whiting, house, barn, shed, $2,450. In 1864: Tyler farm divided, now $67 to $70 per acre, up to the present year. Thus the reader will plainly see that the Tyler farm has always *been taxed.* I shall not refer to the railroad damage on said farm, as words are powerless to show the ignominiousness of the railroad appraisal; it is soon to be in court.

A tribunal where equity ought to reign supreme. The parties in suit are tauntingly assured by the glassware man and his followers, we shall be divested of all in the controversy, as the court is to be fully controlled by the railroad defendants.

A point omitted in my letter of the 17th—A. E. Batcheller building and stand. The building was sold for most $1,000, the town paying $500 for one-half of said building which is now our custom house. The land connected with said building, containing fourteen rods, sold for a little over $5,000. Said land, together with land owned by heirs of Dexter Stoddard joining, was bought by Daniel Whiting, December, 1849, said Whiting paying $100 for the same. Thus the $5,000 lot cost less than $20 in 1849. Also, I stated in my letter that the North Brookfield Railroad would and must ever remain a branch road, because of its grade, or require two engines for constant use, should an attempt ever be made to go west, or north from this route. As the railroad is built, it is and can be clearly shown to be special individual profit. A. & H. Batcheller subscribed for and took $3,000 worth of stock in said railroad. The report has it that said company cleared over $20,000 on freights last year compared with the previous year. Thus you see in ten years (the term the road is leased to the Boston & Albany) said company will accumulate $200,000, besides all other emoluments and ease of which they are the recipients from said road, &c. Other parties are making wonderful strides to fortune in this town, which have been and are so ably set forth by the late glass and crockery-ware drummer. Said business he followed for years, giving him this powerful vernacular over the ignorant and stupid, making them his mere tools for his and a few others' aggrandizement. Nine-tenths of said drummer's report as to the town's advantage in having said railroad is as frail and bawbling as the ware he sold was brittle. As said drummer has changed his business, and is now a manufacturer of ladies' corsets in Worcester, the great advantage he derives from said railroad, as he leaves his family in the morning and returns in the evening, "of course on a season ticket and his family eligible for free rides," as report has it. He and a few others, have reason to shout and cry aloud how great and munificent that North Brookfield Railroad is to us. But, readers, to have your property taken illegally and you made poor individually, and your property a sinking fund to make a few parties' fortunes, and know that the thousands subscribed to the Southbridge Railroad was made by your ruin, is not a fanciful situation.

North Brookfield Town Meeting.

On the 29th of January, 1875, the following articles were acted upon: "Article 2. To see if the town will vote to subscribe for and hold shares in the capital stock of the North Brookfield Railroad Company," &c. "To see if the town will vote to become an associate," &c. "4th. To see what action the town will take in regard to raising money to aid in building a railroad from North Brookfield to East Brookfield, &c. The second article was acted upon first; viz.: "Will the town subscribe for and hold shares to the amount of $90,000 in the capital stock of the North Brookfield Railroad Company;" carried. Third Article, "To see if the town would become an associate for the formation of the North Brookfield Railroad Company;" carried. On the fourth article, the town chose Chas. Adams, Jr., Bonum Nye, and S. S. Edmunds, to act with our town treasurer in negotiating for the amount subscribed for.

Eminent lawyers, in Worcester, have been consulted upon the legality of the above proceedings, and the following is their decision: "The town had no authority, Jan. 29, 1875, to vote to become an associate in the North Brookfield Railroad Corporation, and the subscriptions of Charles Adams, Jr., agent to the town, to the articles of association, and to $90,000 of stock, is void!!" The above decision, which canvasses a law question, has called forth from the *Art Critic* the following, which has been thrust in the burdened taxpayers' face: "The old maids and farmers of North Brookfield have a bastard young one, without a backbone, thrown upon them to pay for and support, at the figure of $90,000."

At the town meeting, June 14, 1875, when it was to give up or proceed in building the railroad, fully half of the audience were boys and unnaturalized citizens, who shouted and stamped uproariously, and did not hesitate to vote when the yeas and nays were called. Thus the vote to proceed to build had more than fifty illegal votes.

The town was pledged to have the railroad fully equipped with rolling stock, and for $100,000. The $100,000 is taken up and we have no rolling stock, but we are paying to the Boston & Albany Railroad $2,000 per year for the use of rolling stock upon said road, which is six per cent. interest of $33,333.33$\frac{1}{3}$-100. Thus the demand for our road was $133,333 $\frac{1}{3}$-100; thus one-third more for equipment.

E. R. HILL.

A VOICE FROM THE CITY OF THE DEAD.

BY E. R. HILL.

[Suggested by the vandal spirit which characterizes the plucking of flowers from cemetery lots.]

Mortals spare these blooming flowers—
  I pray, them harmless save,
To watch through night's long dreary hours
  Round my dark, lonely grave.

Show kindness to these little gems—
  Don't take them from my bed;
More precious far than diadems
  That crown a monarch's head.

Spare, then, oh spare this little lot,
  The only boon I crave;
My spirit lingers round this spot,
  And in its odors lave.

Commit thou here no sacrilege;
  Mourners revere this plot
And deck it with a living pledge.—
  Tho' dead, I'm not forgot.

May all observe the ten commands,
  To break the least one dread,
Then men won't rob, with ruthless hands,
  The city of the dead.

Tread softly—the ground is holy!
  See whose grave she weepeth o'er;
Lo, the simple superscription,—
  Little Darlings,—nothing more.

That's enough! These pregnant letters
  Speak a volume to the heart,
Full of more pathetic meaning
  Than the labored lines of art.

NORTH BROOKFIELD, August 24, 1877.

(Printed in *Spencer Sun*, Mass., August 31st, 1877.)

[*Spencer Sun*, August 31st, 1877.]

WEST BROOKFIELD, August 8.

Mr. Editor,—What's the matter with that North Brookfield Railroad? You seem to doubt that its dividend last year was 2½ per cent. Why, they have a rising young politician over there who figures up in their town report a dividend to the people of North Brookfield of 20 per cent., or $20,000, last year. That young man displays a head for figures that should warrant his immediate employment by the Charter Oak Insurance Company to figure up the value of the assets of that famous concern for the edification of their policy holders. I noticed one day last week no less than six loads of coal going over to the North village from here, and I understand that ever since the railroad was built our dealers have supplied coal by teams from here to the North 25 and 50 cents per ton cheaper than their famous railroad has been able to do. Parties looking at some of the empty shops over there with a view to business, found freights 70 cents per ton on the railroad and 50 cents from depot to shop, or $1.20 per ton, while they found that they could have teams bring from East Brookfield or West Brookfield to them for $1.00 per ton, or 20 cents less than railroad rates. The inducement to locate there to help pay a $70,000 railroad debt was not inviting, especially as the present rate to reach their shop or residence is the same as the old stage coach rate, unless they foot it and back their trunk. East Brookfield seems to be receiving all the dividends declared by the North Brookfield Railroad. Nevertheless the rising young politician expects to declare a 40 per cent. dividend this year (on paper). It is rumored that the declared dividend of last year is to be used to aid the Southbridge Railroad, and the 40 per cent. dividend of this year to build your Spencer Railroad next spring.

FACTS.

[*Spencer Sun*, September 7th, 1877.]

Of the four railroad land damage claims which have been entered in the courts, all but that of Mrs. E. R. Hill are now settled; only one having been tried. No one feels like blaming the directors for their action in relation to rights of way for the road, though there is a general feeling that they made a great mistake in attempting to themselves adjust these claims in the first place, however commendable their intentions. While the town was very unanimous in voting for the road, a small minority, especially those whose lands were to be taken, were opposed. The directors, no doubt, thought to conciliate all these by paying them generously, and even more than disinterested appraisers would be likely to give them, so that when the road should be completed and used, all opposition and local friction should cease. But in this they were doomed to disappointment; for so long as one land owner could make himself believe that he was not rated as high in proportion as some other one, even twice or thrice the value of his land did not satisfy him. Townsmen who had no official connection with the road, and whose attention was not especially called to these land claims until they were in court, freely express their astonishment that the damages were laid so high not only by land owners but by the directors, and they cannot but ask themselves why an acre or two of land taken from a larger amount, none of which was worth for any purpose for which it could be used, more than $50 to $100 per acre should become worth $300 to $500 per acre for railroad purposes when the remaining lands were not damaged in regard to access or occupancy. Should said roads be built in other towns, and it be true that human nature is everywhere the same, the experience of North Brookfield would suggest to all those who shall have such matters to deal with, and who also desire to avoid local friction and the stirring up of bad blood, that they commit the appraisal of land damages to the legally constituted authorities outside of themselves.

My work and improvements are making good progress; I have the gentleman, for such he seems to be, who lives on Jenks' farm, engaged to build, or aid in building, my stone wall, take down my hewn stone tomb built by K. Hill, Jr., in 1858, the stone to be used for underpinning to my L; also to raise my barn three feet or more so that a horse may go under. Said gentleman, and son yoke of cattle and horse were under engagement to work for so much per day till said work was completed; also a cellar wall builder was hired to commence said work one week from Thursday, and to work from ten to twelve days, as the demand for such labor should require. &c. Morse working digging trenches, cutting weeds, cutting walnut trees, as I had marked from twelve to fifteen to be cut for the saw mill, having seen Doane of East Brookfield, and disposed of the same in part, &c. My faithful man accomplishing with his might all he undertook; with my guide and help business was being dispatched. All at once a dozen of men, more or less, made their appearance on *my railroad bed* in my *beautiful* rich mowing, where I was performing menial services that those very men, all but two, were devising, and had been from the laying out of the railroad, to filch me out of my last dollar if need be, to prevent one more cent coming out of their pockets, and most of them recipients of cheap freight, &c., Charles Duncan, Augustus Smith, T. Clark, Hiram Knight, Lewis Hill, *Bothwell* B. Thurston (enough) had told me repeatedly I was offered five times, ten times, nine times what it was worth, as their feelings happened to gull *forth* to insult me, who, in their thirst for riches and to trammel me, were thus arrayed, speaking loudly in words of unmistakable thunder by their way: "You'll g t just what I assess, and nothing more." "Gentlemen of the railroad rapacity, you seem to have much time to devote to reconnoitre, and thus display your consequential ignoramus physics to my disgust, and contempt and scorn, upon my land that you have illegally robbed me of, making me poor indeed." Upon this Bothwell grabs my arm, shaking me as a dog would a woodchuck, saying : " You stop your blab, or I'll put you in the lock-up forthwith," still shaking. "You insignificant, trespassing cur, take your hands off of me." Mr. Morse (colored man), working in agony at the sight of the beastly proceeding : "In God's time, for this assault you will be held amenable." Every man in broad grin at Bothwell's doings *spurs him on*. He grips and shakes vigorously. "We have heard the last of your blab on the railroad, we are gon', too. And you remember, if you"—" *Take your hands off of me*"— "begin to speak of this affair any way I'll have you in the lockup. *Understand me, one time more will put you in the lock-up.*" Bothwell letting go of my arm as the men were on and could not see him, said railroad horde going to my further mowing returned with evident satisfaction at their conclusions. I said : " You left your two-legged dog here while you viewed my land in your custody, which is as a sinking fund to make you wealthy, and have ease and happiness, and to liquidate the rich abundance which my land is productive of to you. The widow's mite would not be given me by your bastard souls." Bothwell, grabbing again (Deacon Thurston in great glee as well as twelve-year, more or less, church-molled Augustus Smith) : "You have got to go into the lock-up!" " Bothwell, if there is an ourang on God's footstool that knows as little as you, I think Barnum must have him. I'll write forthwith and see if Barnum will give you his place, and thus raise some honest money for you!" Laughing he goes on with his gang.

Reader, there are not words enough in the English vocabulary to express my feelings of contempt toward those deacons, church members, friends and members with whom my hard earnings had contributed for the support and spread of the gospel at home and abroad ; men who had always, since their residence in town, (*God be praised they are not natives*) never known me to be anything but one of the most straightforward, unimpeachable females on earth, and they, in their dollar rapacity, are ready to sink me in contumely and shame, to cover their illegal traffic. At my cottage house, for in no other place on earth is such hallowed, grief-stricken association, and in no place under heaven could I stay but there ; where I see my darling boys in every room, constantly loving, soothing, bearing me up with their angel whispers. I bathe in arnica Bothwell's grip plainly to be seen, my frame in agony, physically and mentally, and I cry in anguish, "where art thou, oh God of justice, where?" it's enough to blind the strongest faith, to see such iniquity prevail. I only take a remedial composition, No. 6, and retire before dark. In the morning I rise, sore from Bothwell's rough handling and my hard labor. It is the day appointed to be in Worcester about my monument. I am off. Next day it rains. I rest on my couch, glad indeed for the chance to lie abed all day, more or less.

Rev. Mr. Murray's argument on this last point is mine also.

In Hammersfield churchyard, Suffolk, on Robert Crytoft, obit. 1810, aged 90 :

> As I walked by myself, I talked to myself,
> And this myself said to me :
> Look to thyself, and take care of thyself,
> For nobody cares for thee.

Monday, Sept 10th, business is progressing like a weaver's shuttle. Thursday four men, yoke of cattle and horse will begin to bring to pass my plans for digging cellar under L, laying wall first from the garden lot to cemetery. Brother tells me bloat Bates' brother is dead, relating when he saw him last, and where, and what doing, &c. Another telling still more. The town having been blest with the absence of that posterity as soon as freedom from parental authority would permit—the father dying with apoplexy. The mother saying North Brookfield was not large enough for her children's progress, &c. The mother's mind is much like glassware, and the family are noted for great representations by all. In J. Duncan's words, "they have more wind than brains."

We all present, telling some happy reminiscense (that is laughable), I brought up the rear by saying : Whereas, if it could please Almighty God to remove hence T. C. Bates at this time with his brother, the devil would have a grand span to hitch up when starting on one of his exploring expeditions, "seeking whom he may devour."

I imagine my readers calling for another epitaph.

An epitaph in a churchyard in Seven Oaks, Kent, England :

> "Here lies old 33 per cent.,
> The more he made the more he lent,
> The more he got the more he craved,
> The more he made the more he shaved;
> Great God, can such a soul be saved?"

September 10th, 1877. Robert Morse is trimming my apple trees in front the old homestead—every branch thereof dear to me, because they are of my father's planting. "An Ethiopian could change his skin, and a leopard his spots," as easy as it would be for me to do the same labor anywhere else that I can and have performed upon this my once seven and a-half acres of land, which that Bates & Bachellor Railroad have so hideously ruined for my purposes long since planned. And the slavish labor at my Hill residence, to bring in repairs after nearly seven years' renting to Tom, Dick and Harry. But *that tomb in the garden* containing my once husband's first wife and child, *and our four darling boys*. That house and barn, those grape vines and valuable fruit trees, with their sacred associations, have ever spurred (as Dr. Porter said in his certificate of recommendation, which I would here insert, but it is in the cottage house) my indomitable courage on to repair and keep reverently every token of the above association ; safely guarding every point from the encroachment of the vandals, which in our midst so abound. Still, having sympathy for their needs and giving of my mite as I could, since the ball club rap, my income has been too small for necessary needs, and thus avoid consuming my real estate. Thus, I was laboring with my might, while I was in school, summer and winter, private school spring and fall. My two years' and more feeble health (after ball blow). My land was neglected, only selling its products at standing prices; my purposes, long since planned, are being at this time completed; not being in public school since "said blow;" and normal teacher being sought—brains and adaptation not qualities requisite; for most of the committee are so ignorant, who employ them, and have charge of our schools, and our school mediocrity is apparent as noonday.

Thirty years since, North Brookfield, Massachusetts, was the highest type of morality, virtue and educating power of any town within the radius of twenty miles; and it has been my opinion, well grounded with careful knowledge, that with the number of her inhabitants, her equal is not to be found, in my knowledge, east of the Alleghany mountains, of being the reverse of the above statement at this date; and, it shocks my inmost soul to see its depravity, and also the ignorance and official barbarity which characterize those who happen to hold office—many of said offices being filled with those depraved, low minds, just a grade higher than the wolf and swine. Notwithstanding the great rush to get the almighty dollar, there has been reported one minister of the gospel certain, and maybe two, declined a call to the "Union Congregational Church, because of its querulous spirit, *of which church I was member;* said church I have not entered since March 1st, Sabbath communion, 1872; stating, on leaving said church, to Charles Underwood and others, I never should darken the doors thereof again, till Freman Walker, Samuel Skerry and some others were disciplined according to Congregational usages, in their fabricating testimony against me, &c. The very church I labored day and night, working night after night, without laying my head on a pillow, making pants and dresses—everything to aid, support for said society; waiting upon and providing for sewing circles from fifty to eighty, and for Sabbath School class, parties, &c., as my husband would not permit me the use of his means for such purposes. Thus I labored, thinking it was my duty. Said sewing circle's large ledger book was thus earned, and presented to said body while secretary and treasurer, 1857, '8 and '9. Mrs. Amasa Walker requesting me, on presentation, to write my name, &c., within, which I did; and they must constantly be reminded of me, unless they have *cut it out.*

And the citizens, well knowing I could command and effect the establishment of a private high school, and thus my work of enlarging my house and making preparation for to keep my hired man in attendance the year round. Mr. Haston assists me to-day, and I, reckless of my life, worked with said man to put into the barn this very day, more than ten hundred of rowen cut Friday previous. Mr. Quigley, a worthy, respected man, came into my yard, speaking of the immense second crop of rowen on the Hill plot, and of my great improvements made from time to time.

September 11th.—I can't delve in labor to day. The couch only is a fit place for me. That is Robert's step; faithful of the faithful, his tools are at father's house. I must bestir myself. I'll not stop for breakfast, but hasten down and have Robert remove those broken apple tree limbs (broken off by ice and wind last winter), as they are and have been a terrible eye-sore to me (and it's probable the funeral of the above mentioned Bates will be to-day), and the rough look of those trees shall not mar the prospect of any in said procession in their great display, if it's in my power to remove them. I am on the ground already, the axe is wielding, bringing about my purposes.

I don't see my brother; have you, Robert? Perhaps he is butchering this morning; I will go and see; I find him in the valley of despair. No fire—I set myself to work; brother is clearly discouraged, because he has taken the nominal pittance granted him for his land taken, and would not have complied, had it not been owing to his counsel, etc. Just say to the railroad lawyer you are employing: "Would to Heaven I could here state the way they have managed, but I am going to wait a little longer; each time of action shall be set forth with perfect accuracy." It is high time that this court farce should be ended! Money instead of justice is on the throne!

I got his breakfast, and tried to rouse him with my vigorous talk, etc., telling him I shall cause the banks of New England to smash when my case has a legal adjudication, &c. Then I'll fix up and make great display. As those who have you now cribbed as well as said railroad, they not being able to circumnavigate your youngest sister yet, with all their bought in influences. After breakfast I am hard at work gathering up boughs, &c. It's nearly noon. It has just come into my mind that both outside doors and some windows are open in my cottage. We are holding the ladder to the elm in front of father's house, while Robert stands upon it on the wall; I am in terror, fearing he will fall. The branches are off; I go for bed cord. I go to the house for my shawl, &c.; as I came off those huge door stones, J. Duncan turns his horse right upon me with a sudden jerk; I spring back. "You vilest of the vile, dare thus to intrude upon me as if in mockery to make me move for you, you depraved of all depravity!" Duncan, getting out, handing the reins to a boy with him, boy going back towards the village, Duncan crossing to my bars, front of the house (as the profile within will show the reader), takes hold of the posts and gives them a shake as if to see their strength, &c. "You worse than murderer, you have been told not to trespass upon my premises." He looks at me with a vile smirk that only his mouth and eyes can give—said senses are fearfully vile, in their expression in their best state. I step into the door, and call the lady to look at J. Duncan, the monster of monsters, who used my name to get his insurance, saying I set fire to his building, that his jealous crazed wife and family had been devising to bring about for years. I have heard their threats hundreds of times in her jealous frenzy, wishing the same time every painted-faced widow could be in the midst, &c. The lady looked as Duncan was at the other bar posts with his hand upon them. I say, "See his vile face."

Said building being under an insurance blanket for $2,000, more or less, above any purchasers price would have paid, &c. Mrs. Duncan sending her sons and daughters there in ways various, to watch their father and the "widders"; and scores of times I have heard from her lips, as well as G. Dale, who figured with *whispering voice*, telling the story they had made up and learned parrot-like. Having previously seen in my counsel employed suspicious management, I went to P. Emory Aldrich (now judge), to take my case, *telling him so and so.* Said Honorable duly saw said V., stating my desire, &c. Said V. replied to the Honorable that there had been a misunderstanding between Mrs. H. and himself—he still retained the case and should and did. And my submitting, when I ought to have resisted, caused me, I believe, to lose thousands upon thousands, which, instead of the small pittance given me, would have been decreed me had said Honorable managed my case. Duncan's son Charles has been established in different business with his father's money, and four times failed, at the right time, as report has it, Drury and J. E. Porter, and others, losing from $500, $1,000, $1,500, and so on. The last development set forth in our midst, I heard Osty Hebard relating. Said Duncan would rent weakly carriages, and some accident would befall e'er they were returned to the stable, for which he would get fabulous prices (considering), &c. The carriage repairer and dealer having had fallen out one time, said repairer refusing to bill in repairs, the certain repairs mentioned many times before, saying he drew pay enough on that hole for a dozen carriages. Said Duncan has a son Wendel, and Frank, that will fill the places of the two older members well, if nothing happens to them.

Reader, I will here say, at that court in Worcester, money, instead of truth or law, or evidence, was on the throne, as everything under heaven was done to cover the guilty party, and kill the innocent. Report has it, money buried the criminal, and the ladies that Mrs. D. had wanted to put the fagots about and see the grease fry out of, could be with her, as never before, and many others with Duncan ready for a time, and when she would at home demur, as listening ears have told, he would say "you can't get up another court." I hasten homewards for bed cord, and to shut up my house.

I have all, and lunched, and some for Robert, locked my door and off; ere I get out of my yard, I see a procession; I go back; seat myself in the parlor, at the east window—the only one open in the house—in arm chair; as I looked up *bloat* Bates was looking down on me, looking like a double sunflower, and no more sad, notwithstanding the scene. Seeing my neighbor in sight that I had been in the habit of speaking to, I addressed her, "You see the gamblers' display," &c. Such scenes affect me just as John B. Gough views those scenes since the burial of his mother. Waiting till time for them to reach the yard, I started again, coming out of my gate, the omnibus approaching to bring back *masons;* I waited for it to pass on; and the retinue gone, I make another start, saying, a perfect type of Bates' hinderance, from the time he gained monopoly of the rambling crew in the big shop. On reaching my first mowing, I saw my man had fallen a large walnut tree, and was trimming, As my order, as to the butt, had not been given, I called him, and told him to leave the butt its full length for the saw mill. Robert not noticing, I raised my voice in repetition. I then passed where we were, to be back to the elm tree; two horses were hitched at my bars where I enter, the omnibus being between said carriages and father's house. I turned sideways to pass through,—I could not have gone abreast without rubbing my clothes on the wheel,—saying at the same time to omnibus driver: "Please unhitch those horses from my bars; I wish to pass through, and more, a gambler's horse cannot be hitched to my bars." The driver thought it "d——n mean if a horse at a funeral could not be hitched there." I said: "You please attend to this forthwith; circumstances alter cases; I refuse no one the privilege, except those who have to me committed the unpardonable sin." Willie Stoddard, an epileptic, forthwith commenced damning me. I remarked: "You are a precocious nephew," at the same time untying the horse, not moving the horse, at the post where I pass between the post and wall, said driver having the other horse pushed back; I passed back the same as I had advanced, stepping upon ends of bars beyond the post on to a four feet wall, walking some six or eight feet before I could get down, as the branches trimmed from said tree were between the wall and the tree.

As I was climbing down, I saw two other carriages at my other bars; I called to them, saying: "Gambler Bates' horses cannot be tied to my property." Parties not noticing, I spoke loud to be heard, and none too loud for six rods' hearing; they saw me, and grinned, &c. I got down; in stepping down, I stepped just the right way to bring that hard, painful sensation about my heart which, all who know me at home have heard it described, my hand upon the same as it were to keep it within. Willie ordering those horses tied back with boisterous voice, I going at or near a pile of trimmed branches I was going to pile for sale, when Bothwell's voice was loud, yes, yelling, "Let those horses be, Miss Hill, don't you;" Bothwell running, looking like an escaping lunatic, white apron and gloves and black elsewhere. Willie informing him of my ugliness, he says: "Miss Hill, don't you untie these horses again." "I shall, sir; a gambler's funeral horse cannot be hitched to my bars." Bothwell sprang over the wall like a hound, running to me, grabbing me, saying: "You have got to go to the lock-up", calling Ralph Bartlett and another smaller boy to let down the bars, and the same time shouting for a team to be brought to him to carry Miss Hill to the lock-up; and I tried my best to get from the foul fiend, calling my man. Bothwell threw me upon the ground, resting his knee upon the right side of my bowels and hip, hurting me so badly I screeched with agony, he throwing his right leg over upon my left leg and ancle, grazing the skin six to ten inches. Bothwell shouting to the Furnace boy to come and hold me, also to omnibus driver; I commanding them not to enter upon my land, as Bothwell was violating the statutes, and disturbing the peace; and then he, for the first time, said to me, "I arrest you for disturbing the peace," the Furnace and Bartlett boy roaring with laughter, and Willie Stoddard also. The said three above mentioned carried me and threw me into a wagon like a beast, Bothwell grabbing both my wrists in one hand and at the shoulder pit with the other; when he fastened hands upon me, neither hand did I have till after I was thrust in the felon's cell, in the presence of that vile North Brookfield Ring posse, who were having a jubilee, never equalled among savages. My nephew, Willie Stoddard, following in the advance crowd, "That's good, Bothwell, keep her there; don't let her out at all," &c. The chill of the cell (it being a very warm day, and I in thin three thickness of cambric dress) soon caused me to shake as with the ague; I demanded to be let out; I had forbidden Bothwell thrusting me in there; I resisted in the power of my might. When Bothwell locked me in the cell, he says to me: "I've got you where I want you, and every man, woman, and child in the town will be glad to hear you are in the lock-up; you remember I told you just once more, and I'll lock you up." "Bothwell, I am not here a criminal, a criminal there, nothing else to you but criminal. You will suffer for this false imprisonment."

Bothwell: "Suffer for this false imprisonment. I shall be doubly paid for putting you in." "Bothwell, I warn you to be careful of what you say to me in this felon's cell, for God and His angels are witnesses of your false imprisonment of me in this loathsome hole; your every expression I shall cause to be printed, the full account of which shall be spread as far as any act ever done in Massachusetts." B.: "Now I tell you, Miss Hill, do you dry up. If I hear another word about printing, d—n ye, I'll put the gag on and the handcuffs." Hundreds were without the cell. I screeched for to be let out, as it was endangering my life to be in there. Bothwell says, "Dry up; I'll have the gag on you; who cares for your life? Everybody will be glad to have you die," &c. Bothwell going out, my brother from the homestead came to him and demanded my release. "You have no right nor reason to imprison my sister. I demand her release." Bothwell, grabbing his collar, said: "You say another word, and I'll put you in the other one. Then two cells will be filled." I begged of my brother to go home, thanking him for his good purpose. "Bothwell longs to get you in the cell, you well know. He knows you have been paid by the railroad, &c. Bothwell is after money, or I should not be here." He still demanding my release, I said: "Go home; don't let Bothwell get your money. Remember, Moses, what Mr. Leach says about Bothwell, deficient some $700 to $800 in some store, for which no account can be rendered. Remember Leach says he would not trust him long enough to turn round, and every word of Leach is truth. Don't let Bothwell get your money."

The two-legged bloodhounds gathered thick and fast. The boy who stole my watch shouted: "You are locked up instead of me." Sherman soon appearing that had my hay, not purposing to pay for it before he cut it, as I can plainly prove, laughing, running out his tongue, being of fearful phisiognomy by nature; his son's mouth also stretched with laughter. One-third of that crowd would have been glad to have shouted long and loud. There were boys and girls, who had been my scholars, in tears falling fast. But there were young men of the Christian Association, such as Frank Bartlett, George Lincoln, as they were looking in the cell, and others, who would have stayed me in there till I died before any effort of theirs, I fully believe, because I would not countenance the fraud of their proceedings.

In vain I called for help to release me from my false imprisonment. First, I had not committed any offence but what was my legal right; secondly, I was upon my own land in performance of my urgent necessary labor, and was being stopped in the performance thereof by said crowd, who had halted there purposely (a plot evidently arranged by the railroad men, J. Duncan and masons, before knowing I was working there). Had it not been thus, all the teams at that parade (for such only could it truthfully be called) could have been tied to the posts owned by the town for that purpose. And so far as myself was concerned, I should have as soon stooped and paid obeisance to a *drove of hogs*, my sensitive nature having been previously trampled and outraged in the most atrocious manner by said Bates and Duncan, both those parties having been forbidden, long before this, ever to speak to me or step upon my real estate of which I am legally seized, or lay hands upon its boundary of which I am entitled. I will say here, for the appalling, ignominious crime which said James Duncan had committed against me, the prison walls would be his boundary if it were not for his money shielding him; and his thousands have been in part gained through dishonest traffic.

The last time Bates spoke to me, except the 27th of May alluded to, he told me the "commissioners had offered me ten times as much as my land was worth, but you want to fight, and fight you will, till you won't have a cent to buy grub with." That Bates, who has through the violations of the statutes, taken my property, of great value to me, and thus making said property a sinking fund for his wealth and a few others. Still defiantly taking possession of my entrance upon my land, still making me extra steps and renewed lacerations of my sensitive nature; and more still he has done his utmost to prevent my reporting for papers, &c.—and we never speak. But, readers, you see, he and Duncan are going to do with my property as they wish—law or no law. We are making the money, which will save our necks from any evil we may do, even if the defendant was spotless of sin, as the blood of the Lamb. Back to the felon's cell, in which I am incarcerated by ruffianly design of long purpose in some way or other, to end me, as my knowledge of their illegal proceedings, scrutiny of which is dangerous to their pockets and official wires, if, perchance, law should ever be vindicated. I still demanded my release, as my situation was such at that time, doubly imperilling my health, if not speedy death. Bothwell replying, " Nobody cares whether you are sick, die, or not."

" What Christians you are in this midst. Bothwell, remember every word; it's truth shall be in print." Bothwell: " I thought you were just going to die here." " Perchance my life may be prolonged, sir, to spread this appalling crime you are committing from pole to pole. And the citizens of this town are permitting me to remain in this filthy cell. There are meeting houses within a stone's throw, and churchmen constantly passing, knowing I am here without warrant, without crime." Willie Stoddard shouting, " Don't you let her out; keep her there," &c. Charles Stoddard and some others looking into the cell, I asked them to go to Father Walsh, and tell him the proceedings. Some one says, " Write and I will carry it," &c.; Bothwell saying, "It is high time you had a Catholic praying for you." " I certainly shall ask no one to pray for me—that is my prerogative you have no power over, nor any one else." Bothwell passed out, soon returning with ink and paper, saying, " Write to your priest."

Father Walsh, I have reason to believe, from what I have seen of him, is a man of unimpeachable character. Would to God we had more in our midst.

I wrote my note, said Charles Stoddard carrying it and bringing back a verbal reply. My brother and another man, in a carriage, came and demanded my release from that cell, in the name of the Commonwealth of Massachusetts. Bothwell told him if he repeated it he would put him in the lock-up. The man with my brother, getting out of the carriage, demanded my release also, Bothwell threatening him with a lodging in the lock-up too. Readers, do you see how that ring were playing their cards? I shouted to my brother from the cell, in my utmost screech, "Moses, I beseech of you go home—I thank you, I thank you—you cannot effect anything; don't stay any longer; Bothwell will have you and your money if you are thrust into the cell," &c. Bothwell comes in, saying, "I'm going to gag you. The crowd told me to go the whole figure, now I have got you." "You can put your gag on at the earliest moment you choose. But, sir, God's time for your reward, for this illegal brutality, will come. Not a slave driver in the Southern Confederacy ever committed so heinous a crime as this you and your ring are committing against me, without a cause, but a diabolical plot of Duncan, Bates, masons and the railroad thieves. I ought to have inserted that Bothwell built a fire in the stove at the time of bringing paper and ink, letting me out of the cell into the larger room, where I told all the children to remember me there in that cell without crime or cause. Innocent like Christ, who was crucified by a similar mob, and as Christ was innocent, even so am I. Telling them to remember just how I looked, what I said, and to be telling the same in every different place they are in, that this outrage may spread from pole to pole. "Remember, children, what I say to you here in this felon's cell, tell it to your fathers, and to your children, and your children's children to the third and fourth generations." Bothwell coming in, telling me to "dry up, or you will go back to narrower quarters." My brother at the window in tears, demanding again my release. Bothwell rushing for him, the crowd closed around him, and thus that foul fiend was kept at bay, from putting his paws upon my brother. I said, "Do go home, let not that vile devil put his paw on you again." Others seeing my earnest desire, urged him also. Readers, my brother had not the force to do what he demanded. Had I been in my brother's place, and my brother in the cell, brought there for the same reason, without warrant, without cause!!! female, as I am, I should not have left that spot without his release, and had I been thwarted (as my brother), then and there, that spot would have been made memorable. For Bothwell, or I, would have been numbered with the congregation of the dead. But that mysterious Providence of Almighty God, made me the victim of these money crazed devils, as Christ was victimized hundreds of years ago. There are so few men to be found to-day that dare oppose or espouse any cause if it is going to affect their purse to disadvantage, no matter how just, unless said cause can make a party and give them an office.

And, reader, where, oh where can be found one who would not equal contemptible Peter, who denied his Master, ere the cock crew thrice, &c.

The street lamps are burning. In the felon's cell, Bothwell brings in a soot black lantern and stands it upon the floor, and says to me "You keep your d——d blab going and keep this mob here, or you'd been over to Jenks and home." "Over to Jenks, what do you mean by that"? Bothwell: "Dry up, you will be in the narrow corner. Not another word." So low and menacing, the fiend from the lower regions (*they tell about*) must have stood aghast at thus being excelled. Charles Stoddard, nodding me to the window, in low tone tells me, "Don't speak, they are going to let you out when the stores, &c., are shut up." Gladly indeed, my tongue was silent. Bothwell going in at spaces between the cells. I will here say during the afternoon of my imprisonment, some prominent churchmen and women looked on to rest, and have joy of the same, I suppose—such as Thomas Snell, Rev. Hewes, Deacon Nutting (known as key-hole Nutting), said Deacon being the one who, through said key-hole, criminated Rev. Waldo with Persis Tuttle, of the Union Congregational Church notoriety, bringing continually upon the ministry forever, bonum magnum Nye and daughter, she being very diminutive as well as her father in stature, and far more diminutive both of them in the attribute that is of God. Such expressed eyes as she glanced into the cell, spoke *so loud her thoughts*, and it brought her vividly before me, in the school room (primary department, none other, and for this *never had a certificate or examination; her own words to me*), inflicting blows upon a fat sunny face (Frank De Land), with such velocity as to leave visible marks for more than a week, the marks of her fingers. Mrs. De Land has told that wrong to me, scores of times, and Mary Nye her sister; report has it, the ruler is still to be seen with blood and hair dried upon it, with which she too inflicted blows upon the head of a helpless boy, the boy grabbing the ruler and escaping the school-room with the same.

The last act was committed in District No. 1, North Brookfield, Mass., and the first one in No. 2. About 10 P. M. the streets are clear; previously no one in sight. G. C. Lincoln passes, halts, does not come up to the window, for there I stood in the dark; he soon moves, for fifteen rods more will bring him in Dr. Tyler's office, where the masons can secrete (the doctor having passed the cell in the road, looking straight to his furious steed).

All is quiet in front of the cell. Notorious John Hebard and Bothwell came into the cell, Bothwell having a blanket and Hebard a buffalo, both in broad laugh, Bothwell saying, "knowing you are a clean devil, I bring you a clean buffalo." Hebard: "Ha! he did this d——d nice." I screeched as loud as my voice could ring for help. "You cannot leave me thus endangered, without defence, with these two men, and Hebard's known additional trait. I said to Hebard, "I am not in this felon's cell as a criminal, but by the malicious designs of men." "That's a d——n great get up. I have come in here purpose to see you here, that I can—ha! ha! and tell of you wherever I am." "Tell, sir, of my innocence,—of this fearful, loathsome den." Hebard: "God, you are d——d innocent." "Sir, if justice was meted out to you, as report has it, heaven is my witness (I know nothing of your guilt but your *presence*), you, sir, with said milliner, as current report has it, would long since be in prison from violation of God's law as well as man's." Hebard: "Well, you would have been in hell with your d——d back broke. I wish to God I could have the chance of breaking it and chucking you down."

I still screech for help to rescue me from thieves saying, "Even as Christ hung upon the cross between two thieves eighteen hundred years ago, to-night in the nineteenth century, I stand between two thieves as innocent of crime as that Saviour upon the cross. Bothwell coming back of me as you would drive a dumb beast into a stable, saying, "You go into your bed." "You are not going to shut me in that cell to-night? I must go home." Bothwell: "You won't go home." "I tell you, sir, the foul fiend from the bottomless pit would not be so insolent and audacious. You have me here without warrant, without cause, and I demand you no longer break the law of God and man." Bothwell takes out a paper, saying it's a warrant and he will read it if I say. "When was it made out?" "This evening." "What is it made out for?" Bothwell: "For your disturbing the peace." "It is you, and you alone, with your called comrades, that have disturbed the peace, because I did not surrender my property, my individuality, seating myself in the imbecile's chair for you to move, and step upon as the circumstances of the ring may demand." Hebard: "You're a d—d good horse block." Bothwell: "I tell you, go in that cell." "I go, sir, if you dare drive me in there." Bothwell: "D—n you, I do dare—" I advancing in the door of the cell, when both men put their hands with force upon my back, sending me to the further end of the cell. The cell is locked. Hebard: "Pleasant dreams all night—it's too d—d good a sight to leave." Both, in high glee, gone out.

Soon Bothwell comes in, and asks me if I want anything to eat—a cup of tea? "I wish, sir, to go home, and change my clothes, and rest upon my own clean couch." "You won't; say, do you want a cup of tea?" "No; I wish some ice water." "You can't have it. I'll get you a cup of tea"—at the same time shuts the sky-light. I beg of him not to, in vain. He is out—gone. My throat at that moment was parching. Since my diphtheria sickness, in 1864, I have suffered with dry mouth and throat; and, having talked much, and some of the time loud, in the cell, to make those without hear me, had added to my suffering thirst. Often in my rheumatic sickness, there is no moisture in my tongue, and in my best health, I am often obliged to drink with every mouthful of food. Imagine me without food or drink, but one glass of water since 11 o'clock, A. M. My sufferings from thirst alone, were fearful. I stood in the felon's cell, both hands on the middle bar, leaning first one shoulder then the other, against the bars—the rheumatic pains sharp and piercing—watching the dim light from the street lamp; and, as the town clock struck from time to time, the only society except for Duncan and Hebard stable, and when hearing parties in said place. Also, as I thought, in Burrill's furniture establishment, Burrill and Charles Duncan seeing me many times in the cell, Burrill's daughter having been my scholar, Charles Duncan having upon his parlor table a valuable Bible given him by Sabbath School, in 1866, I should think, towards which I gave seventy-five cents of earnings sewing that I could not earn three cents per hour, and my son Lloyd contributing twenty-five cents towards the same, his earned equally laboriously. You will remember, readers, my saying my husband opposed me in this, and no aid could I have from him. And I thought I was right, and doing God's will, Lloyd helping with willing alacrity. giving of his hard earnings as freely as water runs down hill. Thus those very churchmen were walking by without one word said for my relief, but were, without doubt, as glad as Hebard and Bothwell, but had more sense than to make themselves hideous. Perchance, a human soul within the cell might bear witness. About 2 o'clock in the morning my thirst and suffering was so great that it seemed as if death would end my sufferings before daybreak. On the first step upon the walk in front of the cell was a man with a lantern.

I tried to call, but I could not speak loud. My hand had not let go its grip upon the iron bar, and I believe had death come in that awful hour, my hand would have been clinched tight to the bar. About 5 A. M., Bothwell came in and unlocked the cell, saying, "Go home." I could not move but with the greatest effort, Bothwell saying, "I will get a team for you." I said: "No, walking will be best," he giving me his arm for support; we thus left that awful stench cell. On the street we met Burnett and across the street was Kibby. I have omitted one important point. Morse, my man, came to the cell in the evening, bringing me a shawl and the keys to my house. His agony was intense. Bothwell took the keys, saying he would put them in his watch pocket. Chas. Stoddard, being at the prison window at the time, told me I was going home. I did not object to his keeping my keys, and when he left me next P. M., he said he was going after a cup of tea for me. I supposed he meant what he said. He did not return with the tea. My home was some fifty rods from the lock-up. On reaching home he unlocked the door; I went in, and Bothwell returning. I passed up stairs, thinking for the first time of his (Ernest's) shawl, still on my shoulder. I opened my front door, calling him back to take the shawl. Bothwell came back saying: "I forgot to tell you I shall be down after you to go before Jenks; you keep this shawl till all is finished up." "What, I can't go up; you can't take me there, nor fool me any longer; I have suffered enough, and I must take to my bed." Bothwell: "I'll come down toward night; you keep the shawl." "I'd rather you would take it now, as the smell of that loathsome cell is in my clothes. I shall go into the barn to remove them." Bothwell said: "You keep the shawl," &c., and was gone. I go back to the kitchen, remove said clothes and take a regular bath in wormwood, my body and limbs a sight to behold from the bruises upon my bowels and hip; his marks upon my arms, and my left limb spoke plainly of the fearful abuse I had received from his hands—assaults, and from his foot and knee. I have seen men throw down a dumb beast, and not the brutality ed toward them as he dealt out to me.

In getting my clean apparel I fo d my $450, that was placed in that drawer, lying in full view—the $100 bill, $50, one package of $100 not broken op n ; the $100 in $10 bills had been torn asunder and $70 taken.

I had paid J. B. Lawrence & Co. $110 for a black walnut set, placed in my sleeping room, the week previous, taking only $100 from said package. Said money I had drawn from savings banks spoken of before, one of the firm of J. H. Clark's store in Worcester being witness to the same. Said money was to be used in making repairs, &c. Thus, my lock-up had cost me, by being stolen, $70, besides the unparalleled abuse and outrage of the law.

Bothwell had my keys with him during the night. My doors had been open from 7 to 11 A. M. But it must be evident that any thief, to have entered in the morning, would not have divided the spoils. No, reader ; an old hand at the business performed that job, I think, in the night. "If Mrs. Hill misses it, we can say she has lost it," and so on—their old way of talking against truth, immutable as God himself. I dressed for Worcester instead of the bed, having the appearance of a corpse mangled by a ruffian, and breathing again as if in defiance of death. My brother's presence added force to the new lease of life. "Bring, Moses, the first instant you can, a team, and take me to Worcester." " I will do what I can." Off he goes. I bathe my limbs again in wormwood, my head, also my shoulders, and I am just barely able to move about. Time is money. He comes. I'm off ; and in front of the homestead we meet that wonderful nephew and sister of primary education, and teacher—all her knowledge being confined to North Brookfield's school and ball-room. Willie hastens to Bothwell, as report has it, and reports that Tyler was carrying Mrs. Hill off, &c. My brother, meeting a man with fleet horses and buggy, asked him to take me to Worcester ; said man was going to N. B. on business ; I turned, saying : "Whatever you ask to take me shall be paid." He told me, and I paid him. I had not been in his buggy but a few minutes when I slept; he held me with his arm around me. I told him my short story in his buggy. He said: "Why wasn't that Bothwell killed, and stopped?" "It, sir, would only have been justice." In about two and a half hours I was at Friendly Inn. I went (after eating some refreshments) into a lawyer's office, then to two other legal parties, showing my bruises, &c.

The counsel did not comply with older wisdom and my wish, but so and so. I was too weak and suffering to argue, but had new distress at his not doing as required. And I believe the train from North Brookfield had a passenger that had informed said counsel of the breach in the law, &c., telling him to do his best for their protection by staving off, and the after proceedings proved it to a demonstration in my mind. Home again, so nice, so quiet and pure—and those little angel whispers, so sacred in this hour; no mortal tongue can assuage grief like those angel boys. I bathe in wormwood, in clean apparel; my rich couch has my bruised form.

This morning, about nine, I am at breakfast table. Bothwell comes in. "I've come for you to go up to Jenks," &c. "I protest, sir." B. says: "You have got to go up," &c. "I go with you only to avoid a scene. I protest against it, remember," &c. Bothwell appoints the time, 2 P. M. Leaves. Soon he returns, saying, "Jenks wants to go to the Democratic Convention, and he thinks you better have counsel and have it hushed up. No one shall come into his office except witness," &c. Gone again. I am off again to Worcester for said counsel; too weak to use my own judgment. He thinks so and so, "but you do as you please." I demand the action brought on my part. "Oh, that will keep as it is. And it will be kept from his handling." *He* takes fifteen dollars— will be up at ten o'clock A. M. to-morrow. My man is at the depot with carriage; takes the legal man, brings him to my house. We drive to the grounds; back to Jenks' office. Had it not been for Bothwell's promise that no one but so and so, I would not have appeared before Jenks any other way than to waive examination, knowing his every trait as familiarly as the alphabet. A schoolmate boarding one winter at his home, when teaching in our home district, 1867-8. But thus doomed to have lie upon lie, lie upon lie, to take me this way, that, and the other. Jenks' office was packed. J. Duncan with his vile, lusty face, with fiendish grin. I immediately explain his profile to said counsel. He withdraws suddenly, though his name was offered as a witness. The imps of hell cannot exceed that man in lying, as he has falsified against me, and that lying to cover the vile life he has led. Many say, be careful, be careful, when I have been held as a States prison convict without one particle of anything to lay to my charge, but my knowing how his wife and he quarreled about women, and my living with them in the same house; it could not well be otherwise—and family school teacher. What I have ever said I still say, it's God's truth, and the party who burned his building could have been proven plain as noonday in my opinion.

Reader, this book is in part to speak of this in print to live when I am in the grave, as no justice was given me in court—this court costing me some $600 more than I received back—and had it not been for a man on the jury from North Brookfield of Jane Dale and Duncan notoriety, the pittance allowed would have been more.

Bad witness for Bothwell, &c., but a good one to spread a vile lie. Said Duncan and Bates were talking and laughing uproariously during the time the farce court was pending in Chas. Duncan's store, Bates' *brother* not being *under the sod* two days.

Bothwell's testimony alone, every word he uttered, the way thereof misrepresenting, giving the lie to what ought to have been told in truth, and I tell it in truth.

Hiram Bartlett making himself perfectly ridiculous, idiotic almost, in thus trying to injure me and help said Bothwell. The lawyer was unable to get one sentence from Bartlett. "He heard my voice three or four times, &c." Once he heard "gambler," once "grave," once "d———n." Not one sentence could be brought out. "He only knew I was disturbing the funeral, &c." Esq.: "What else did you hear that made you know?" B.: "Heard me say d———n distinctly." Esq.: "You call that swearing?" B.: "Yes, sir." Esq.: "That's all?" B. · "Yes; I could not distinguish; I heard grave, clear." Esq.: "Then you think Mrs. Hill was swearing like a pirate?" B.: "Yes." Esq.: "How long have you known Mrs. Hill?" B.: "Always." Esq.: "Did you ever hear her swear before?" B.: "No, sir." Esq.: "Mrs. Hill was on her own land at the farm?" B.: "Yes." Esq.: "You think 'gambler,' 'grave,' and 'd——n' were heard at different times, as you state, is enough for you to affirm she swore like a pirate?" B.: "Yes." Esq.: "Questioned every way and not one answer that could be made into testimony." Esq. says, "There is nothing more, sir, as you are evidently laboring under some infirmity—sickness or imbecility, or some perverse freak dethroning reason, judge, nothing more," &c.

Reader, that man wanted a deed of my land, thus to secure me against J. Duncan's vile proceedings. I told B. if Duncan could get hold of my land through his rascality, I wished to see the performance, &c. Bartlett had an eye to the seven and a half acre plot, and could not get it. Bartlett had told me sundry things about those J. and C. Duncan's. I summoned him to court. In ten minutes after summons he was at my house, with his eyes glaring. "What did you summon me to court for?" "To tell sir, that you rehearsed to me the other day." B.: "I shan't go one inch, and make me lose business." "You need not, sir, and you will please never speak to me again on earth. But ever remember the hard work I have done for you in your poverty, and had it not been for my father's house, and Dr. Tyler's, and with my own timely aid, you would have been carrying a saw-horse and ax, instead of pulling teeth." And now for an incident of this H. P. Bartlett when a boy some four years of age. I was playing school in my father's great kitchen, my brother Albert and said Bartlett scholars. For seats my brother's little chair, a very large pumpkin, a very large, crooked neck squash. Calling the lads up to the desk to give me their names, Bartlett, the youngest, pushes ahead of Albert, rapidly saying, as if afraid he would not get his name in first: "Pierce Bartlett Hiram." Albert bursting out in a loud "ha, ha!" Thus, some time before exercises were in order, with book in hand H. P. B. rises, goes to Albert and demands, "Me have chair!" Albert says, "Why, I am oldest, Me have chair!" I said, "Albert, let the motherless boy have the chair." Albert rose and sat on the pumpkin. Not one minute after H. P. B. was at that seat —" Me have pumpkin." Albert rose, laughingly, and sat on the squash, and with q·ick time H. P. B. : " Me have squash, too." Reader, the child is the father of the man. And the three words at different times may have something beside grammatical relation, &c.

To show more fully some incidents in said Bartlett's life when in his teens. C. E. Jenks, now trial justice, by two recommendations is teaching school in District No. 1 in North Brookfield, Mass. In said school were children from the Bates, W. Hill, and Bartlett families. An insurrection rose in its midst, when Bates, said Bartlett and Hill, &c., levelled Charles E. Jenks, carrying him out of the schoolroom. Readers, you can well understand those three names above alluded to, who were going to have their say and way " fair or foul"!!!

And it is just so yet   *   *   *   *   *   *   *   *

The omnibus driver did his best for the trespassing criminals, but failed entirely of giving any testimony of any low remarks or illegal proceedings as alleged by the criminal officer who had caused this disgraceful public trial and false imprisonment of me (Elizabeth R. Hill). This crime of S. Bothwell was more damnable in my heart than *murder*. And his motive and all those concerned was and were to ruin my reputation, thus making me a public show, to suppress my influence in vindicating the law and statute proceedings in which I have been drawn by their illegal desires and proceedings as plaintiff, and they defendants.

Henry Sampson seeing Bothwell's proceedings chanced to hear gambler, grave, &c., God and his angels, curse or damn. Eqs. D. did you hear anything else? I saw Bothwell, and imagined, &c. Sampson was very cute and very near a cypher. John Dewing alone giving any sensible sense and not one word to criminate. Bothwell's testimony was a fabrication of his own making, of which his whole soul teems with, I believe. Counsel asked the above witnesses how long they had known Mrs. Hill, &c? Some all their lives, others thirty years or more. Counsel: Did you ever hear Mrs. Hill use profane or obscene language? Witness: Never. Counsel: Mrs. Hill is a literary lady, so-called? Witness: She writes for papers; is a school teacher; I don't know as she ever wrote a book. Counsel: Mrs. Hill is called literary? Witness: She writes and teaches. Counsel: Don't you know her, and is she not known to have the knowledge and command of three or five times the vocabulary of words the best of us handle, and knows just where to use them? Witness: I know she has knowledge.

Not one witness corroborated Bothwell in his statement, &c. Many others in that procession have told the truth that I did not disturb by calling to the further bars not to hitch to the same as they were much nearer to me than Bothwell and heard nothing, and consider the treatment Bothwell gave me as uncalled for, cruel and outrageous.

My only witness, Robert Morse. Counsel: You are under the employ of Mrs. E. R. Hill? Witness: Yes, sir. Counsel: How long? Witness: I helped with Mrs. Ayres' span and mowing machine, &c., to get her hay the last of June. I have been working the past two weeks only drawing a few loads of coal as Mrs. Ayres wished during the time. Counsel: You were at work at the time Bothwell seized her on her own land in the performance of labor in which you had been engaged? Witness: Yes sir. Counsel: How far off from Mrs. Hill? Witness: About ten rods. Counsel: Did Mrs. Hill do or say anything to disturb or annoy the solemnity of a funeral procession? Witness: No, sir. Counsel: Was Mrs. Hill on her land when the procession passed? Witness: Mrs Hill had been working there all the morning and had gone up home in haste to lock her doors and get a bed cord to tie back a tall elm tree to straighten it up, &c. Counsel: The funeral procession went to the churchyard while she was gone? Witness: Yes, sir. Counsel: Was Mrs. Hill gone any longer than you expected? Witness: Yes, three times as long; she said she was coming straight back, else I would not get through in front of the house till she came back, as Mrs. Hill was going to sort the limbs for sale herself. Counsel: Where did you first see Mrs. Hill when she did come back? Witness: In the highway in front of where I was cutting a walnut tree. Counsel: State what she said, &c? Witness: She told me not to cut the butt of the trees at all, but come and help me tie back the tree as quick as you have the branches off. Counsel: You had cut down a walnut tree during her absence? Witness: Yes, sir, and more too. Counsel: Where did Mrs. Hill go? Witness: To that elm tree in her garden lot where she was piling up wood. Counsel: You had not started to go and tie the tree back? Witness: No, sir, I had not the limbs cut off. Counsel: Tell what you heard next? Witness: I heard Mrs. Hill call me to come and help her. Counsel: I saw Bothwell and the omnibus driver carrying her out of her garden lot. Counsel: Did Mrs. Hill scream? Witness: Yes, sir. Counsel: What did you hear her say? Witness: She said, " God and his angels forbid such outrageous treatment. Bothwell, I forbid you carrying me off my land; you have no cause, no warrant; a more damnable proceeding than this never blackened the pages of history." Counsel: Did you ever hear Mrs. Hill swear? Witness: No, sir. Counsel: How is it about working for her? Witness: I never worked for anyone who treated me better; prompt in paying my wages; kind, and careful of my health, &c. Counsel: Did you see Mrs. Hill in the cell? I carried her my shawl and her keys; I saw all I could; it was terrible to me. Counsel: Do you know she was imprisoned without law or cause? Witness: I do.

Mrs. Hill's Evidence.

Counsel: Mrs. Hill, state your case in full? Mrs. Hill: I was directing and working as usual, with Morse, my hired man, the day of the funeral alluded to. Hearing that it was to be that day, I made great exertion in work to remove brush into heaps and pack cut branches to give neatness, for perchance a stranger may be in the midst of the coming display, and hastening work I had long before desired done. I had no thought, nor passing notice of the proceeding (" it was none of my funerals"), but was accomplishing with my might, fearing my wood cutting, &c., would not be completed o'er my team for dragging stone, laying wall, &c., would need Morse in their aid, &c.; I had not lost one moment, but to bring to pass, except to answer the profound queries of nephew Stoddard, &c., and I had silenced him in a measure (as talking and physical labor are not unitable in my caliber), by informing him, that he should be my guardian, if I could be permitted to choose, &c., and then he could question and direct as "seemeth him best." When I came out of the house at the homestead, to go home for cord and shut my house, I should not have noticed who was in that team had Duncan not turned the horse in my face, compelling me to jump out of his way, &c.; when dressed in farming gear it is my practice not to see or notice passers by. Duncan's movement I have given before in this book, was pre-arranged. Bothwell's carrying me, &c., to the prisoner's cell, was planned and arranged to be executed in some way by said rings, &c., with as much deliberation as any plot of iniquity consummated since God made man! The previous mentioned acts, and the concluding one to be given, cannot help proving to the candid mind the iniquitous designs of those two legged, moral depraved, and money crazed species of manhood. I find I have omitted a prominent point. I solemnly declare that I did not speak in any way to disturb the funeral; furthermore, had that procession been anything but outside show, they would not have seen me at all. I did not move a horse, nor put my hand upon horse or carriage; I merely untied the hitching rein at the post, which is foot passage, between post and wall when not thus obstructed. I did not remove the rein from post hole. Omnibus driver having unhitched the horse at the other post, I leaving the post and going to the other. Stepping upon the ends of the bars up to the top of the wall, &c., then seeing my other bars being taken, I spoke, telling them not to hitch there; for reasons before given; they not noticing, I repeated louder, to be heard by the parties, and not loud enough to be heard by said procession in the grave yard. I had not, previously to the burial, nor since, stepped toward, nor looked at said spot in said yard, though the most sacred of all places; but I never knew of a public place but there was an avoidable spot to some one, and such spots to me I notice not, I turn from them, and turn away. The lies told of and about me in this affair are as foul as hell, and are a perfect type of the character of those who promulgate them, and they spread the same through impish maliciousness.

Counsel argued the case ably, setting forth each testimony in its true light, the audience manifesting a slight applause by clapping and stamping, whereupon Bothwell rushed upon his feet with maniacal authority, saying, I command every one to leave the hall this minute—I command every one to leave this hall! But the court objecting, Bothwell at the same time taking hold of one and another, pushing them along out of the hall—Jenks and counsel trying to stop him, saying he must not do this, the audience have done nothing to be driven from the hall—counsel declaring he will not be thus disturbed, &c. Bothwell gives in thus: You may stay 'till there is another clap or stomp. If there is one stomp you shall every one leave the hall. Selah! How would it have been if that applause had been for and as favoring his vile, worse than murderous proceedings? Can you imagine?

The counsel goes on, makes out Bartlett imbecile or under some derangement, or he would not have thus shown to all such open, barefaced, incoherent words, without one connecting word, thus hoping to criminate innocence. Though I should perhaps have said to Mrs., don't object &c. You all well know how keenly alive Mrs. Hill is to the least insult from Duncan since her court against him for slander, &c. And Bates, you well know their position, and when Mrs. Hill says bloat Bates she means bloat Bates. I never saw bloat Bates, but I know he is bloat Bates, for Mrs. Hill has thus affirmed.

As for Bothwell's proceedings I shall say nothing, and I trust the judge will have nothing to lay to Mrs. Hill's charge. My mental agony and my paid counsel leaving Bothwell thus! That treacherous falsifier! worse than murderer! not analysed!!! The chief actor and cause of this scene, as much as the devil presides for imps in the bottomless pit. Oh, oh, oh, oh! was my mental ejaculation. Jenks stammering worse than when I wrote his will (he once sent for me at the school house about 2 P. M.; I immediately hastened to the rescue, as he was blue and thought he was going to die, &c., Wm. Wright witness and somebody else. He will have to make a new will as three or four are dead, else this secret would not be divulged here, saying), I guess as things are I must give Mrs. Hill $15 and costs. And, readers, that was said not because there was sin, but because he must do it to keep his office!!! I appeal, and Jenks then says, you may go under $300 bonds. Such hideous mockery of justice! That last insolence calmed me; oh how calm I looked at those malefactors with as clear an eye of their diabolical determination to rob me of money, to crush me in spirit, to thus hold me forth to that or this blaspheming, taunting throng. A more ignominious set hell could not purge from its bowels. Bothwell, in glee: Who will you have for bonds? My brother would be bonds, you have a mortgage on your place, &c. (not covering one-third of it). I said, can't I give my own security? Jenks: No. Counsel: I think you might let Mrs. Hill be her own security, as she owns property, pays taxes and always lived here. Jenks: That makes no difference. Another man came forward, worth his thousands: Jenks, don't your wife hold the deed of your property? Yes; but I am worth a good deal more than that, you know. Some parties, because they had not back-bone, like that contemptible "Peter" and others, left. I looked round and said: The audience cannot fail to see this bend in this proceeding, and I will here ask in this way, if there is a man in this hall who holds real estate, free from incumbrance, of sufficient value to secure said bonds with my brother; qualifications not publicly known, not much account anyway, nor likely to be, come and administer the cup of cold water, if such a man can or must be found; no other will be admitted here; or else I shall have to be remanded back into the felon's cell where the parties are making aim for. Forth came a man I never laid eyes on before, and if it was to save me from the pit I have never been able to call his name, he having to designate his property, where situated, to Bothwell and Jenks. A Frenchman—God bless him! and reader, "how is that for high." I will say I sent runners to call in DeBevoise, Avann and Wilson, ministers. Wilson was present, DeBevoise absent. He only is seen to help crime in its deepest dye, as I will hereafter name.

Bothwell immediately asked my counsel to go with him to see about property. My paid counsel considering it. I consider it an insult to rush him from me at this moment. Counsel well understood that move won't work. Down in the carriage, drove home. Recess: at noon of one hour counsel dined at my residence, also driving to the homestead a second time, counsel advising me not to cut any more walnut trees (without his advice being asked.) I had an internal smile, reading thus: you think you can keep the case so and so long and be sure of pay.

Oh such management of courts! It is enough to make drops of blood burst from my face, knowing as I do their proceeding. We returned to Jenks' office, as counsel had left his coat there, I in the carriage with the driver. The loud ring of laughter from those three men, the length of time it took him to get back to the carriage and his frail excuse, planted him, never to be resurrected, in my mind again, mentally saying I have paid you, take you as a gentleman and return you to the depot. Good bye forever, so help me God.

The day before said Court I posted the following notice upon the Town House, beside the box for public warrants, &c.:

"Owing to malicious and designing abuse, from citizens of this town, I am compelled, for my own safety, to issue the following:

"Whoever trespasses upon my land, bars, gates or wall—that is, boundary line of the real estate of which I am legally seized—will be held amenable to the law.

"Dire necessity has caused the above to be issued for the safety of my being. "E. R. HILL.

"NORTH BROOKFIELD, Sept. 10, 1877."

Bothwell, taking from my hand a poster, saying I will post one of these on the Adams Block. Said Bothwell posting said poster low down on a barber's pole, as report has it. Neither poster to be seen next morning.

> "In memory of
> Mr. Rufus Herbert,
> Who fell in the bloody
> (Committed by Benedict Arnold's troops)
> Massacre at Fort Griswold,
> Sept. 6th, 1781,
> In the 40th yeer of his age.
>
> Reader, consider how I fell--
> For Liberty I blead!
> Oh then repent, yo sons of hell,
> For the innocent blood you shead."

NORTH BROOKFIELD.

The town is excited over to-day's trial of Mrs. E. R. Hill for attempting to break up a funeral procession. Theophilus Bates, having hitched his horse to her fence while attending his brother's funeral, she unhitched it, and when it was again tied, treated the whole crowd to a tirade of indiscriminate abuse. Being arrested, she threatened to undress and appear clothed only in her native purity; but as this didn't seem to terrify the constable much, she thought better of it, and contented herself with loud talk and threats of burning the houses of all the Bateses and Duncans in the place. She is known in the town as a woman of considerable mental power and a most fearful temper.—*Springfield Republican, Sept.* 14.

Mrs. E. R. Hill, of North Brookfield, was fined $15 and costs, Saturday, for disturbing the peace, but appealed and was put under $300 bonds to the Superior Court. Her husband asserts that the prosecution is malicious and that the arrest was in violation of the law.—*Springfield Republican, Sept.* 14.

NORTH BROOKFIELD, September 18.

Mr. Editor,—As you have repeated in your last issue the atrocious libel which the *Springfield Republican* issued against me, for the special benefit of the North Brookfield Railroad Corporation and Masonic aggrandizement, seemingly hoping to adjudicate the railroad land damage to which the parties are defendants, on whom their wreaking thirst for my land, my character, my all, must have satiety. Mr. Bothwell's throat to Mrs. E. R. Hill, when settling for services, viz: J. Duncan and wife slander trial, in March, 1872, which my memoranda will witness. He too has had a cup of satiety which he wishes to drink from at my expense and character. Said Bothwell, on the 11th instant, in open violation of the statutes, trespassed upon my premises without cause, except the above mentioned, and without justifiable provocation seized me on my own land, while in performance of my daily labor, &c., holding my hands and calling help to hold my feet, and thus I was carried and forced into a felon's cell about noon, and there kept in that loathsome cell till 5 o'clock the next morning, full report of which, together with the taunts of himself and John Hebard to me in the cell, will be issued in pamphlet form at an early date, if my health will permit, together with profile of grounds, &c. And every statement in said book shall be "the truth, the whole truth, and nothing but the truth, so help me God."

E. R. HILL.

NORTH BROOKFIELD, Sept. 21st, 1877.

Rev. G. H. WILSON,
    Of Union Congregational Church, North Brookfield,
    Mass. :

I herewith send you protest as minister of the church above mentioned, forbidding your administering the "Lord's Supper" to S. Bothwell, member of said church, as he stands a perjured liar before Almighty God and man, by the testimony he fabricated on the 14th inst., against me, on whom he was wreaking his long thirsting revenge, together with the taunting throng, who are, as of old, ready to blaspheme virtue and purity.

Respectfully,

ELIZABETH R. HILL,
Member of said church.

NORTH BROOKFIELD, Sept. 21st, 1877.

REV. G. H. DEBEVOISE:

Gentleman,—I herewith ask you to cut the walnut tree standing upon your grave lot in Walnut Grove Cemetery, in said North Brookfield, Mass.; my grave lot, which is holy ground, ranging by side of yours, A. Barlow and R. Doane, you three gentlemen owning said lot and trees thereon, which are a nuisance in said yard. I have repeatedly been eye witness to married men, women and boys, throwing clubs upon said DeBevoise tree to bring down walnuts therefrom, to my grief and horror. And according to agreement made heretofore, there is, on Tuesday next, a valuable monument to be placed upon my holy lot in commemoration of my loved, lost, beautiful boys, upon top of which is a biblical symbol; some parts thereof may be easily broken by boughs, clubs or sticks falling from said tree, ignoring, at this time, what may happen by malicious design in thy midst, of whom, in church, you are "head shepherd". Therefore, I pray you, without delay, even before the setting up of my monument, bought, marked and paid for, you will cause said tree to be cut down at once.

Respectfully,

E. R. HILL.

I delivered the above letter personally to Mrs. I. May (wife of cemetery committee) and in whose house said DeBevoise rooms. On my way there I called at the store of G. C. Lincoln, second selectman of said North Brookfield, and read to him, orally, the above letter, asking him to forward the cutting of the above mentioned tree (at

March meeting the selectmen were appointed to act with the cemetery committee in removing said trees, laying out of new lots, repairing tombs, building wall, &c.). He commenced arguing thus: "We can't do it; Mr. DeBevoise don't want it cut, and we shan't cut it; and you need not try to make any fuss about it; it'll amount to nothing but one of your rows." I sarcastically replied: "I did not stop to argue, only to notify and appeal to you as an officer of the town." G. C. L. said: "Very well." I sped off, and ere I reached said May's I met said Committee May; reading the letter to him in the street, to which he replied as follows: "That's right, and well explained, and Mr. DeBevoise and everybody can tell just what you want done; it ought to be done; the trees are a nuisance, and we committee did our best to have those trees cut when felling the rest in the spring." "Will you 'tend to it?" "Yes; DeBevoise is not at home, but will be at one o'clock P. M." I went on and left said letter with May's wife, to be delivered on DeBevoise's arrival without delay. The 22d, eight o'clock, I was at post office for my morning mail, and there found a postal card from monument dealer stating my monument was being delivered by private team as the safest way and would be at Walnut Grove Cemetery between eleven and twelve o'clock A. M.

As I turned to come out of said office Mr. DeBevoise stood at my right hand. I said, "Mr. DeBevoise, my monument is coming up this morning," placing my card before him, pointing at the time, &c. DeBevoise very pertly replied, "What is that to me?" I says, "Did you get my letter yesterday?" DeBevoise: "Yes; I shall do nothing about it whatever; that tree will not be cut." Hill: "Mr. DeBevoise, all branches that encroach upon my lot from said tree will be removed this day, as they are a nuisance; if you will cut them it will save me the trouble," I following him to the door, DeBevoise repeating, "I shall do nothing about it," in tone and manner that brought forth the following: When returning from Uncle Thomas Bartlett's, Plymouth, Mich., in 1873, I was on the express train following the one whose baggage cars were precipitated in the Welland Canal, near

St. Catherine's, and while workmen were removing the wreck, baggage, &c., detaining said train some five or six hours before the bridge could be let down, that the train might pass over, I saw what I called some very diminutive, ignorant French Canadian (Cannuck) men; but I don't believe there was one among them that possessed so contemptible, ignominious a spirit as that which earthly Gabriel H. DeBevoise has just manifested to me, the "widow and fatherless."

In going home I passed Mr. L. Brewer's (cemetery committee and honored sexton), calling, leaving my letter to said officials, which was written at the same time of said Gabriel's, telling him what my card at hand informed me, asking him to proceed at once to execute my complaint and wish, Brewer replying it shall be seen to at once, taking the letter addressed to them, and starting forthwith. I will see the committee, and it shall be 'tended to. I have tried for years to have all those walnut trees removed, for they have always been a nuisance in the yard, as you say. And a more objectionable one there was not than DeBevoise, going out of his saloon in advance of me, I following, saying, "Your committee will be down there without fail at said time, or early in the P.M.; you know I am all alone to tend to this sad business." Brewer: "Some of us will be there." I passed home, put on my working apparel, went to the old homestead, from which said yard was sold to the town, And at the appointed time said monument arrived, and the colored teamster having been in said yard other times for similar business, called upon said Brewer for cemetery key, and was directed by him to G. C. Lincoln, above mentioned, for the same, both asking if he had Mrs. Hill's monument. Reader, imagine me in that graveyard, anxiously looking, and wondering why don't some one of those men come down here as promised. Three o'clock P. M. the cottage monument was set, nothing remaining but to place an urn with handles (I should think, some 16 to 20 inches high) upon the top, the crowning emblem, said workmen advising me to remove the branches referred to before the setting of the urn, for the liability of said urn being broken from branches falling with the wind, say nothing more, before twenty-four hours, as I had during their time there anxiously watched the expected coming committee, and their non-appearance, caused me to employ them to remove said trespassing branches, which was effected in less than a half hour of time, all refuse therefrom cleared away. Then said men fastened the sacred emblem to its place, I remaining, and with most scrupulous neatness removed, with brush and hand, the most trivial specks ; thus I left. The next morning being Sabbath, I went down about five o'clock to see if all was well there ; nothing being disturbed I returned to my bed, and gave up, sick with rheumatic attack. About eleven o'clock my brother, who lives at the homestead, came to my residence, informing me that he had just driven eight or ten boys from my walnut and apple trees upon which they had been shaking and gathering, the foremost of said boys being the one who had stolen my gold watch from my recitation table in July, 1875. Being in bed trying to sweat myself, I asked him to tell Wilder Dean, Cons., to come in and see me, which he did, Mr. Dean promising to take charge of the boys, and also see that there was no further trespassing upon my real estate. Mr. Dean said he would bring those boys referred to to justice, at once. Said Dean having an excuse for that day, Tuesday also, and Wednesday another excuse, telling me to go to Capen, Brookfield, &c.

Reader, I will now bring forward Gabriel H. DeBevoise. He did not preach to his " own flock " the Sabbath following the trimming of his walnut tree on his grave lot, but said desk was occupied by the Oakham pastor. Monday morning, in good season, said Gabriel starts his legal investigation, as report has it, this wise : By getting the selectmen—graveyard committee—to view the trimmed branches; appealing to them for succor in this bereavement; telling them, unless they proceeded to execute judgment against me, he should be obliged thus to do. The committee having been heretofore anxious that said trees should be felled, as they were destructive to the good appearance of the yard, as sticks and stones were left upon lots by those who had gathered the nuts therefrom, beside the fearful blacking stain, defacing and spoiling all marble under the shadow of said trees. Reader, if you have ever read "Ginx's Baby," or "Dame Europa's School," you may be able to draw a parallel. Therefore, said body informed said Gabriel they would convene Monday evening, and see what steps to take to appease his disturbed feelings. Meantime, said Gabriel began to collect evidence. Calling first upon Mr. M. Tyler, at the farm-house, whom he addressed thus: "Do you know who trimmed those trees in the cemetery?" Tyler: "I don't know anything about it." Gabriel: "Did not you furnish the ladder and tools, as accessory to it?" Tyler: "I did not, neither was I consulted about it in any way." Gabriel: "Could your ladder be taken, &c., without you knowing it?" Tyler: "No." Upon this, Willie Stoddard, an epileptic, came to the rescue, with the following information: "I see Miss Hill and Dennis Horrigan carrying a ladder, saw and axe, and bed cord into the cemetery; the white man sawed off the branches, the colored men carried them away, and Miss Hill cleaned up; I watched um." Gabriel, turning to Mr. Tyler, saying: "You are forgiven." Tyler: "Forgiven for what?" Gabriel, hastening onward, every step bringing him nearer that sanctuary where he preaches "Peace and good will to all men," and "if thy brother trespass against thee, forgive him seventy times seven." And ere he reaches that "dedicated plot," he stops, calls for Mr. Erasmus Haston, and questions him thus: "Did you lend Mrs. Hill tools on Saturday last?" Haston: "I did." Gabriel: "Who borrowed them?" Haston: "Mrs. Hill." Gabriel: "What did she say?" Haston: "She wanted my best axe and saw; she keeps no such implement, and when she wants one, I let her, or whoever comes for it, have it." Gabriel: "What did she say she was going to do with it?" Haston: "I don't think she told; she was in great haste." Gabriel: "Who brought them back?" Haston: "A boy." Gabriel: "What boy?" Haston: "I could not say certain, but I think it was a Horrigan boy." Gabriel: "What did he say?" Haston: "If anything, it was thank you." Gabriel: "Have you seen

Mrs. Hill since?" Haston: "I have." Gabriel: "What did she say?" Haston: "She said her monument was set without accident, and she was much pleased with it; she was here after her milk." Gabriel: "Did she not say anything else?" Haston: "Yes, she wished me to bring her over a peck of potatoes." Gabriel: "Was that all?" Haston: "Yes" Gabriel passes by the next house, being the one from which the dead bodies of wife and child had been borne some three years previous, to whom Mrs. Hill had carried a large quantity of Baltimore belle rose buds, wax flowers, yucca blossoms (baby DeBevoise, though eleven years old, was thus called), together with her brother James, had been my pupils, at my residence, as well as in the school-house, passing the sanctuary to his boarding-house. In the afternoon, G. H. DeBevoise takes a team, drives out one and a half miles to School District No. 7, takes said Willie Stoddard to said school-house, and there calls for Dennis Horrigan; said boy, eight years of age, appearing at their request; and Gabriel questioned him thus: "Is your name Dennis Horrigan?" Dennis: "Yes, sir." Gabriel: "What did you do for Mrs. Hill last Saturday?" Dennis: "I helped her carry a ladder down to her baby's grave lot." Gabriel: "Where did she put it?" Dennis: "Beside her babies' grave." Gabriel: "What else did she do with it?" Dennis: "I don't know; I was in a hurry to get home." Gabriel: "Did you carry anything else?" Dennis: "Yes, sir, I carried a saw." Gabriel: "Who carried the axe?" Dennis: "Mrs. Hill carried the axe and bed cord." Gabriel: "What did she say she was going to do with them?" Dennis: "She did not say." Gabriel: "What did she talk about?" Dennis: "Why I don't know." Gabriel: "You do know?" Dennis, "Why she said the rounds were a foot apart in the ladder, and asked me to guess the distance between things." Gabriel: "What else did she say?" Dennis: "She told me to hurry home, and she would make me a present one of these days." In the evening, Mr. Brewer said the committee had thought it best to have a final decision upon that vexed question.

Sept. 25.—Tuesday morning, report has it, the following

gentlemen were deputized to investigate said monument dealer, and, if judgment could be executed, to do the same. May, of cemetery committee, Gabriel H. DeBevoise, S. Bothwell, who with dripping glands was anxiously waiting for time to speed its flight that he could grasp Mrs. Hill's hands. " I'll get the handcuffs on this time; I tell you we'll get her name in the newspapers, and everything I can have suggested will help bring about the time when she will beg me to let her rest. I'll give you a clear title to every possession of mine on earth. This is the richest thing out, DeBevoise is going to settle that railroad claim for the town." Thus that diabolical S. Bothwell must overflow his peculiar channels of imagination.

Sept. 26,—Wednesday morning, at different corners of the street, report has it, "Mrs. Hill is arrested; DeBevoise done it this time; that French Gabriel ain't going to help Mrs. Hill, 'cause she don't worship deviltry." Just think of that DeBevoise, only a few weeks ago, taking the part of a drunkard, who was profanely and fast driving a horse on the Sabbath day—to such an extent of brutality, that the horse died in a few minutes after he landed in the stable. "That's so. Yes, and that ain't all. When Hebard had the drunkard and horse-killer arrested and brought up in Jenks' office, that little DeBevoise got right down side of Jenks, kept whispering, and, ye see, the feller was almost dead drunk. The horse was an awful sight, he had sweated so. You see, Jenks was obliged to fine him, with costs., and DeBevoiso *paid it.* This will show up old DeBevoise."

Wednesday I was near sick-a-bed; it's not much use to try to move. Mrs. John Weatherel is to be buried this P. M. I went to the homestead, hoping to see the sexton, that I might tell him to occupy any hitching places there are around my land, as I had no objection, and was glad to assist all in their time of trouble, who had not committed the unpardonable sin.

When at baby's grave, Tuesday, I was told of the company that had gone to Worcester, also that Perry, the new sexton, was saying, " If Miss Hill has cut those branches one inch shorter than the law provides, we shall have her arrested;

and we calculate we shall get the cemetery fine on her." Bystander: "Why, Perry, you have been trying to have those trees cut; you're going to join Gabriel in his meanness." "We don't propose Mrs. Hill shall do our business for us." "Why didn't you come down then? You always come when sent for by anybody else. I will tell you why you did not come. You knew well those branches would have to come off over Mrs. Hill's lot, and your committee thought you would hang back, and let her trim, thus making her a 'cat's paw,' to give you the chance to cut those trees down."

Wednesday P. M., I was at the homestead, waiting for the funeral procession of Mrs. Weatherel, and as friends were gathering in the grave-yard, I sitting in front door, Bothwell and Foster rode by, hitching their horse upon my premises; also W.lder Dean, three constables in their working suits; soon followed by Mr. Stone, in carriage, from Hebard & Duncan's livery stable alone; he seeing me, dropped his eyes, as if moist, to weep. Reader, the damnable *plot of these men was clear to be seen by me.* Thus I sat noticing their every move, not forgetful of the sad rite being performed. I had placed in my Walnut Grove plot a cross, with notice reading as follows: "Rev. G. H. DeBevoise, pause and consider. Please, G. H. DeBevoise, preach from this text next holy day,—Upon this cross was nailed a *Serpent*, whose head I had bruised in the path between G. H. DeBevoise and my grave lot."

Fearing the chalk marks would soon be effaced I wrote Rev. G. H. DeBevoise to please preach from the above symbol the next holy day. This notice also on the cross:

"Owing to malicious and designing abuse from citizens of this town I am compelled, for my own safety, to issue the following: Whoever trespasses upon my land, bars, gates or wall that is the boundary line of the real estate of which I am legally seized, will be held amenable to the law. Dire necessity has caused the above to be issued for the safety of my being.
"E. R. HILL."

Bothwell and Foster read said notice, from appearances. Bothwell sitting upon my wall after reading and writing off the same. During his writing he would stop and pick upon said cross (plainly to be seen), thus removing said serpent. The mourners were dispersing, and Bothwell's comrade directed his attention to me in the door. He slowly took himself off of my wall, then turning and coming unto where I was standing, in the presence of scores, and addresses me thus : "I have a warrant for your arrest for cutting those trees ; I ain't going to read it now, but I give you a chance to get you a lawyer, as you will be tried before Jenks, on Saturday—so be ready." I did not speak. All eyes were upon me. He continued, "I warn you not to cut, or break in any way, a limb or branch hanging over the wall on your land. The wall belongs to the cemetery, and the limbs don't hurt your land ; if you cut or break one I shall have another arrest on you, the warrant is in my pocket to do it," &c. Still I did not speak. Bothwell said : " Will you be ready on Saturday at ten o'clock?" Still I did not speak. Bothwell said, "If you are deaf and dumb it's no use to talk," and walked off. Reader, I did move, after he passed, and went east to look and see what Bothwell had picked from the cross. He had picked the serpent off, thus removing the symbol so significant at this time. Miss Horrigan came along, carried me home, and then went to the village for my mail where I heard of the most fiendish plot being laid to end my public career for all time. One said, " last evening, so and so, was arranged for to-day, and you have outwitted their design, it's only added fuel to their flames. I tell you, Mrs. Hill, *if you should not speak in your ordinary tone upon railroads, or your imprisonment in the cell*, they are going to get you there, or into some hellish spot." I still breathe, but, readers, I say to you that never, in ancient or modern history, or in works of fiction, can be found printed the *malicious designing abuse those church masonic men are dealing out to me*. Reader, you cannot think it's the cutting of less than one-half foot of solid wood from the three trees; oh, no. It's their *sins*, and Mrs. Hill *will not compromise* the same. Thursday morning I went to Worcester, and there learned from a monument dealer that the men described came into his building, Tuesday, and asked him if he cut the branches for Mrs. Hill on Saturday; and as he did not, and the two men were absent, they were not likely to find much satisfaction. He described a short man with stove-pipe hat as nervously snapping and moving all the time. I says to myself, "I wish that little spitfire could let off some of his fuel, he'd feel better." Reader, that little man was Gabriel.

Sept. 27.—Thursday evening I returned home. Ere I could get there, I was told " they had been drumming citizens to be at the Town Hall on Saturday, for Mrs. Hill was to be tried before Jenks; don't fail to come; tell all the boys; a gay time we shall have; golly, I guess she wishes she hadn't wrote about the railroad," etc. And a good churchwoman had read something her own fancy had suggested, and the frail gossip women were gathering together, hoping Mr. DeBevoise will get the case, he is so good; he ha'n't had a chance to play croquet once (this being Gabriel's pastime). Mrs. ——— says, "I think it is a shame Mrs. Hill should dare cut those branches!" At my own home, soon my bell rang, when a friend came to me, saying that Bothwell had employed, as report says, a fish-pedlar to spread my arrest, and trial to be on Saturday, and to tell every one to come on for a time, and the pedlar has done so! Readers, this book represents the condition of affairs in North Brookfield, Mass. Saturday I was in New York city. Sent telegram to C. E. Jenks—" I waive examination. Call on Erasmus Haston and T. Horrigan for bonds. Elizabeth R. Hill." Thus, that Saturday DeBevoise was thwarted in his evil purpose against me. Reader, I would no more go before Jenks and the tools the town uses to maltreat justice and right, and utter a word again, except the above dispatch, than I would put my head in the largest live hornet's nest ever seen by man, and expect to come off unstung. I wrote Tuesday (on hearing of said gentleman G, being still on the raid) to cemetery committee, to refresh the mind of DeBevoise of the number of times he had thrown refuse upon my land, also trespassing himself and son many times upon the same which may be applied as follows, "An eye for an eye, a tooth for a tooth." I will here insert a few epitaphs.

On the tombstone of Rev. Joseph Moody, a somewhat eccentric pastor of the olden time, at York, Maine, is this couplet—

"Although this stone may moulder into dust,
Yet, Joseph Moody's name continue must."

At Banbury churchyard, Oxfordshire, England, is the following:

"To the memory of Ric. Richards, who by a gangreen first lost a toe, afterwards a leg, and lastly his life, on the 7th April, 1650.

"Ah! cruel Death, to make three meals of one!
To taste, and eat and eat, till all was gone.
But know, thou tyrant! when the trump shall call,
He'll find his feet, and stand when thou shalt fall."

The following is said to be on a tombstone, near London:

"Poor Marthie Shiel has gone away:
Her would if her could, but her couldn't stay;
Her had 2 bad legs and a baddish cough;
It was her two bad legs that carried her off."

The epitaphs can be used as a comparison, if you wish.

The following inscription on a tombstone, in England, may be regarded as somewhat doctrinal:

"Bold Infidelity, turn pale and die—
Beneath this stone four infants' ashes lie;
Say, are they lost or saved?
If death's by sin, they sinned! because they are here;
If heaven's by works, in heaven they can't appear.
Reason, oh! how depraved!
Revere the Bible sacred page, the knot's untied:
They died, for Adam sinned; they live, for Jesus died.

That Gabriel H. DeBevoise was held as eccentric by his own parishioners, by others, simple-minded, and many hoping he would know enough to leave town (by being called) without being advised he must go, &c. I would wish to call the name, but will at the time it may be desired. During those many hearings, I never spoke against him. But I will say, within the last four years, at funerals, he has astonished me beyond measure, and his great notice of parties having perpetrated demoralizing and prison offences. The first case I will mention is Fred. Porter, who was obliged for illegal misdemeanors committed in Boston, where employed, being at the time twenty-seven or eight years of age (as I have been acquainted from his birth to that time), and, if report is true, not the first nor second but third offence (Mrs. Paradize particularizing to Mrs. Josiah Whiting, said Paradise associates, in Boston). He leaves, nobody knows, *as is told*. After being gone twelve years, more or less, returns last summer to his mother's house. During his absence he changes his name to Perry, marries, and is a father. Thus his wife knows nothing of his home but that he is an orphan. He returns to his late father's house, his wife, Mrs. Perry, and the child, Perry. That's the way. Well, how is it, Mr. —— ? Reader, is that child's name Perry or Porter?

The late Dr. Porter, not on noticable terms with said Gabriel DeBevoise, and when DeBevoise's child and wife died, Mrs. P. with her own tongue, hoped it would be the means of Gabriel removing from our midst, &c. She hoped he would know enough to understand its plain meaning. He has not sense for the needs of this town, &c. When the prodigal son returned, Gabriel was foremost in giving him front rank, so far as his influence could avail, inviting him in the church with a rush (a disgrace). When I called on Gabriel (reader, I never shall know Rev. to that man again) informing him of Sherman, etc., said Perry or Porter, wife and child, was at his office; Gabriel urging them to call often and play croquet. When I left said office, I wished him to visit me. Gabriel replied: " I will see Mr. Sherman; I think he ought to pay you, and if you will not enforce the law, I will see it is paid." I told him I had no desire to deal in law; far from it, &c. All the words since between DeBevoise and me, are in this book. DeBevoise was going past my mowing that the engine had just set burning. I directed his attention to my trouble. " That " says Gabriel, " won't hurt it any; that, there, and then a 'balm in Gilead!' "

The reckless driver and killer of a horse on Sabbath day. The Monday following, Gabriel was staving off jail for said criminal, and truly rehearsed by the "boys here before." Another instance of moral depravity in our midst, and Gabriel figures: Thus, a miss of twenty years and more, born of common people, which money had advanced beyond good sense, was about to be married, having six bridesmaids and six grooms (in waiting). She became ailing, &c., and calling a sugar-pill doctor, his prescription was: "Be married without delay." Her innocence she declared; also denying if it was that, she never "knew men." The affianced groom saying, "if it was so, it was not his; he had never 'known' her." She doctored and doctored, and the sugar-pill urging her to marry. Her sickness brought wonderful rotundity. Said sugar doctor went to Dr. Tyler, as report has it, to go and see said patient. Dr. Tyler, passing out into the sitting-room to father and mother of said girl, said: "If you want your grandchild born under wedlock, my advice is to have your daughter married this evening; the child will be born inside of a week and prepare for the same at once. Good day."

The father, daughter and to be-son, started off in haste, going to South Brookfield, calling their minister up and out of bed, and, without maid or groom, were married between 9 and 10 o'clock P. M. Oh that fearfully lying to a mother, hypocrisy to be handed down from generation to generation, is the greatest destroying sin of this world. That affair was laughable. The big shop promising the child pegging-block or piano. It is what I call low, but shows the color of North Brookfield. Gabriel evidently sorry (by his conduct) that she had to say, "I am sorry I have sinned, and I pray this church to forgive us;" all is now white as snow; drive on.

There was a lady, good-hearted and a good singer, died; Gabriel was much affected (it seemed as if he would burst), and also it seemed by his calling Mrs. Stoddard so often, so near together, that his grief thus found vent. A lady, aunt by marriage, was so disgusted (as well as many others) she hitched this way, that, and the other; if the turns had been straight ahead, she would have been a number of rods off.

I have laughed many a time till my sides ached, thinking of his fanciful eulogies, and his great power of giving those who are pleasing to Gabriel their local position in heaven. Gabriel calls forth this epitaph, on a tombstone near London —

> "Here lies the body of Nancy H. Gwyn,
> Who was so pure within;
> She burst her outer shell of sin,
> And hatched herself a cherubim."

Another leading singer died also, Milliner. There were mourning gossipers—" let us go and see to this funeral," and Gabriel was more extravagant beyond decency to those who knew her whole life and he, to make such mockery to the truthful minded. is an outrage upon truth. An epitaph will conclude this :—

At Sarragossa, Spain, is the following :

> "Here lies John Quebecce, precentor to my Lord the King. When he is admitted to the choir of angels, whose society he will embellish, and where he will distinguish himself by his power of song, God shall say to the Angels: "Cease ye calves ! and let me hear John Quebecce, precentor of my Lord the King !"

Near San Diego, California, a tombstone thus reads :

> "This yere is sakrid to the memory of William Henry Skaraken, who caim to his deth by bein shot by Colts revolver—one of the old kind, bras mounted and of sutch is the kingdom of heavin."

Last summer Charley Belcher died, 18 years of age, a scholar of mine, a son of Temperance. Gabriel presided, reading from his book of selections, one passage, " In our Father's house there are many mansions," Gabriel had a thought strike him, then and there, thus : " that even in Heaven there was a place for Charley," &c. I retired behind my handkerchief, and his remarks brought to mind, "Then you do think the Almighty will let Charley a three-legged cricket, or small-sized cigar box to squeeze in somewhere, perhaps." Gabriel always has his special, fancied friends. Charley, I knew, was prepared to meet his God in peace, and Gabriel disgusted me there. Mrs. Porter has often told of a certain member of his church saying his funeral poetry—it seemed to her, as he stretched them on and on, like bobbin on the tail of a kite. Reader, I hope the earthly Gabriel will profit from the above, if Congregationalists will countenance him after a knowledge of the following proceedings, written in this book:

Thursday. Sept. 27th.—At Worcester, Jenks, Nye, Bates, Bacheller, in the cars, happy as angels of "darkness," I noticing every look, wink, or wag.

At Spencer, before Worcester, to see about publishing the railroad proceedings, which are herein mentioned. I am told that North Brookfield "wants this affair hushed up." I'll be your bondsman for that! The way it will be hushed on my part will be to print in pamphlet form their illegal diabolical proceedings, and thus spread the same from pole to pole. I expect to be murdered by that gang and mob, but God grant the delay of the same may be till the truth has gone forth to accomplish that which cannot be reached in our courts, now in custody of money and not law.

At Worcester, to see and have my profile altered, as promised, and bars and trees arranged by exact measure by the surveyor of the plan of the map herein. "Said surveyor is in the south-east or west part of the State," I am told by the clerk. "As said place is somewhat latitudinal, can't you tell when he will be back from that large place?" "He will be gone about three months, engaged; he will be on at times." "Please tell him I was here to-day for him to put bars, &c., on the map, as he agreed to do willingly and readily, and expect him to do the same, and give reasons for your direction of his whereabouts, which to me means cents on the eyes."—Gone.

In less than one hour after reaching my own house in North Brookfield I was on my way back to Worcester; baggage—a change of under-clothes and one extra basque.

Saturday, Sept. 29th.—I am boarding at 91 Sands street, Brooklyn, N. Y. Having made all arrangements for printing pamphlets, and having made part payment before leaving, telegraphing, and telling in every place my fugitive condition, sympathy and listening ears to every word, and it has proven there was not a "Judas" among the crowds of audience. But "God assist you!" came from many a lip.

Many pages of this book are written and given to the press, and God grant that every line may accomplish that for which it is heralded, and bring reform out of chaos, light out of darkness, is the prayer of

E. R. HILL.

E. R. HILL,
Sept. 29th, A.M., 1877.
At Westminster Hotel (for I am a fugitive, confidentially), New York City, N. Y.

(Telegram.)

C. E. JENKS,
North Brookfield, Mass.

I waive examination. Call on Erasmus Haston and T. Horrigan for bonds.

ELIZABETH R. HILL.

E. R. HILL,
Oct. 8th, 1877.
At Western Union Telegraph Office.

NEW YORK CITY, N. Y.

(Telegram.)

DISTRICT-ATTORNEY STAPLES,
Worcester, Mass.

Put over my appealed cases. It is *impossible* to be present.

ELIZABETH R. HILL.

October 13*th*, P. M.—In New York City, searching all newspaper offices for Massachusetts news. I am at last directed to Geo. P. Rowell & Co.'s newspaper agency, and, calling for three last issues of Spencer *Sun*, Mass., I find the following:

"Mrs. E. R. Hill's barn was discovered to be on fire on Saturday evening by the engineer on the 8.30 P.M. train. An alarm was immediately sounded, and the engines were promptly on hand, but it was past control when they arrived, and all they could do was to protect the house. It was the work of an incendiary, and the selectmen have offered a reward of $500 for information that will detect the criminal."

(Telegram.)

NEW YORK CITY, Oct. 13th, 1877.

To Dr. WARREN TYLER,
   North Brookfield, Mass.:

For God's sake protect my house, and all therein, safe.

ELIZABETH R. HILL.

Reader, in this sketch-book I bring forth facts which exhibit individuals who are figuring for my weal or woe, as you may see; and the unavoidable inevitables which the wickedness of men have hurled me into are mysterious and appalling; still they come, fiery, fierce, causing a wail of woe to burst forth, arising from the very citadel of my being. "What meaneth it?" I point. "Mrs. E. R. Hill's barn was discovered on fire on Saturday evening by the engineer on the 8:30 P. M. train. An alarm was immediately sounded and the engines were promptly on hand; but it was past control when they arrived, and all they could do was to protect the house. It was the work of an incendiary, and the selectmen have offered a reward of $500 for information that will detect the criminal."

I am Mrs. E. R. Hill—oh—oh! the cup runneth over; I am a fugitive from that, my native place, by *that ruthless mob which you see are still rampant*. The extract is cut for me from the paper; I pass out in the street writhing in despair; I *see* a policeman; I ask him to show me to the telegraph office; with all kindness I am aided along. Oh, my God, wilt thou protect me from that unsatiated railroad, masonic frenzy. Gliding quickly to the table, I despatch, "Dr. Warren Tyler, North Brookfield, Mass.—For God's sake protect my house and all therein safe—Elizabeth R. Hill." At the delivery, "How soon can I receive an answer?" "About ———." "Please send reply to 91 Sands street, Brooklyn, *my place of abode—confidential*—I am a fugitive here from a plotting, intriguing ring who are hunting me down far worse than any blood-hounds ever read about in the Southern Confederacy."

At the same time showing my "extract cut from the paper," "Are you insured?" nothing worth, compared with loss. "We will deliver your message when returned, in haste," I passed out; asked policeman to aid me to Fulton Ferry. I pass through the crowds in the cabin to the platform; the wheel has stopped rolling over head (laying cable), but the ponderous wheel in the deep will soon roll me stilly across the river, while the surging billows within heave moaning like the ocean that cannot, cannot rest. "Saturday evening," those plotting fiends bent on crushing me in every conceivable way! The chain is unlocked, the wheel moves, stilly, noiselessly I am gliding o'er the waves of the deep, while the waves are surging mountains high in my soul!! "All they could do was to protect the house." My house must be riddled; that barn only nine feet from the house, with over five tons of hay of the very best quality in every way, nearly half a ton of coal, the rest outside in a bin there; my barrel of Henry Ward Beecher's sermons, my barrel of *Christian Unions*, my barrel of Educational Journals, and other periodicals that I have been gathering for the last eleven or twelve years; that pure, dry hickory wood and piles of barrels and boxes; that barrel of pure cider vinegar, three two-gallon jugs of the same; would that mob smell of that vinegar in that hot flame? My fruit trees, that yield from $40 to $80 per year, must a good half of them be ruined, at $100 or $125 insurance, I know not which. Oh, they meant to burn everything, Mr. Haston, there they could not refuse the engine. Oh, all that mob are sorry for is that I was not in the centre of those flames, just as they had, in olden time, John Rogers!!

Where did my white doves fly to, for safety from those flames?

The time is not now the "dove" can carry the news. I am landed on the shore. Oh, my God, when, oh when, shall I be landed, safely protected from that infuriated mob! Oh, how much street dodging, each one is on his way but me! Oh, God, Thou knowest it is not my way. Is this Thy way? At my nice quiet city home I ring; little Lotty opens, I kiss her through the thick veil. In the back parlor (that's my rent paid for room), on my couch, and a fountain of tears flowing from my agonized soul; oh, my burdens seemed more than I could bear before!! Bella H. is at the piano in the front parlor (her usual place while waiting for tea), it comes to my ear from her fingers touching those keys, "Sweet hour of Prayer," as if God himself had directed her for my need! It soothed and calmed my spirit to rest. It was near nine o'clock before I went down to the dining-room, and there rehearsed my tale of woe!

This notable day is October 13th—I came to this house September 29th. Thus two weeks have passed in Brooklyn City.

October 14*th*.—I try to rise from my couch with leaden weight, affliction chaining me down. Oh, I cannot, I cannot rally from this added shock! Oh, my God, help me! Guide, oh, guide me! Thou Great Jehovah!!! Little Lizzie H., at the piano singing and playing at this instant:

> Pull for the shore, sailor, pull for the shore!
> Heed not the rolling waves, but bend to the oar:
> Trust in the life-boat, all else will fail,
> Stronger the surges dash, and fiercer the gale;
> Heed not the stormy winds, though loudly they roar;
> Watch the "bright morning star," and pull for the shore.
> Pull for the shore, sailor, pull for the shore.

That wave of despair that was surging mountain high to engulf me in its bosom—thus that little ministering angel *stepped forth and stayed the billows.* I rose and wept with joy for this sudden calm. Oh, true, how true, it is said, " Of such is the kingdom of heaven ! "

The two letters written 30th ult., to friends in North Brookfield, not stating at that time my place of abode, though in the very same parlor, and chair, for reasons why, you well know.

To-day I write two letters to North Brookfield, one to Spencer, one to St. Catherines, full of anguish, but suppressed by the above " ministering " Lizzie.

O my pamphlet ; with this new woe to hinder me getting my proofs together, oh, what a fiery link this ! help ! help ! Thou my only Guide ! Mr. Hutchinson takes my letters to post. A tall, thin gentleman, of *very few words ;* but how he speaks : " Madam, be comforted ; be thankful those terrible men did not have you consumed with your buildings. Go on, finish your book, that it may preach from pole to pole." (" Mrs. H.") Write Mrs. Hill, write a longer sermon, than that little French De Be. will preach to-day, to die with utterance. Yours, to help emancipate the world.

October 15th, 2 *o'clock* A. M.—I will try to compile a few more incidents ere I reach the most atrocious savage cruelty ever given to a human being, in what is termed a civilized town. The tears still flow to think of the devastation of my quiet home, where I have labored with my hands with great skillful executiveness, where three of my children, boys, were born, sickened, and died, working in the power of my might for the best interests of mankind, in church, sabbath school, my absence from either was notice of sickness, contributing to the needy in every position of life, without asking how, or what, or which way. Through what or which society can I promulgate my name best that I did so, and so ?

(Telegram.)

NEW YORK CITY, Oct. 16, 1877.

To E. HASTON & L. P. DE LAND,
  Insurance Agent, &c.,
   North Brookfield, Mass.:

Shield my house and contents from the insatiable fiendish mob.

        ELIZABETH R. HILL.

Mrs. E. R. Hill is reported to be stopping in Canada.

(Telegram.)

NEW YORK, Oct. 18th, 1877.

To LUTHER P. DE LAND, .
  Insurance Agent,
   North Brookfield, Mass.:

Is my house burned that contents were removed? Answer immediately.

        ELIZABETH R. HILL.

Not one answer sent!!! My first telegram was to be sent to my place of abode *confidentially*, as I was a fugitive from my native town, North Brookfield, Mass., driven by the Railroad-Masonic-DeBevoise mob. Never was a slave in the Southern Confederacy hunted down by bloodhounds with more brutal ferocity than the rings above mentioned are seeking to destroy me—morally, mentally, physically, financially!!!—all to cover their own sins, and to get the dollars.

        ELIZABETH R. HILL.

Strangers are very kind—their sympathy evidently helps sustain me in this awful hour!

        E. R. H.

October 20*th.*—A letter from North Brookfield. I kissed it over; I well knew whose pen had written that message. I stayed long reading, and telling the ray of hope just come that, perhaps, some of my sacred relics, and earnings of myself and eldest son, were saved to me a little longer, that I may look upon some token of the loved, lost, ere that fiendish mob, by some agent of their own number, will end my life, as Abraham Lincoln. "Oh, lady; not so bad as that, I hope." They will not stop till it is done! They meant to take my only home, knowing well I had no money to replace my loss, the insurance not being one tenth the loss!

The many that have heard my fugitive story are anxiously watching the news when it comes. To every one I show my letter, and its contents read.

Across the river, I rapidly reach my home. Letter first in the hall taken by Mrs. H——. "News from Sodom?" "Yes; but from that one that is, 'peradventure, to save the city!'" She says my barn was burnt at 8 o'clock in the evening; the house not harmed; crowds were there, and on the Sabbath day the hay, &c., burning till Monday. Oh! my God! wilt thou not, as of old, through thy omniscient and omnipresent power, bring him forth unmistakable, to meet that *justice he* so richly deserves. I feel, I know, as if God himself had told me, it is direct from the DeBevoise mob's disappointment. Oh, God! hasten "Thy time" to bring that fiend to the same dwelling where Sampson now resides, who burned George Tyler's barn at West Brook, Mass., 1875, because he was refused a glass of cider (my great grandfather's barn)—4 to 6 fat oxen, 30 tons of hay, pigs, sheep and fatlings, besides working horses, and no insurance.

Sunday, Oct. 21st, 5:30 A.M.—There's that black cat, that ate my beefsteak for me, yesterday morning. How stealthily she moves; she climbs the railing on the piazza, her white paws upon the window pane (so like white gloves); that white paw feels for "that entrance," her black nose touches the glass, with white paw aiding her, to her utmost stretch, showing the white breast (so much like a white apron); she can't enter; disappointed, she climbs down the railing, *scenting, I will find something.*

Black cat, with white paws, and breast, you remind me of the treatment I have and am receiving from some citizens in North Brookfield, Mass.

October 23d.—This morning, at Pettingill & Co.'s, I find the following:

NORTH BROOKFIELD.

The barn of Mrs. E. R. Hill was burned Saturday night by an incendiary, and her house, near by, was saved by the firemen only with great difficulty, loss $300, partly insured. Mrs. Hill, the only occupant of the place, was out of town at the time. She was to be tried by Justice Jenks on Saturday, on the charge of mutilating valuable trees in the Walnut Grove Cemetery. Constable Bothwell, who has held a warrant against her since last Thursday, but did not arrest her, as she was supposed to be a home body, and not liable to be called out of town, only notified her to appear on Saturday. She was in town on Friday, but on Saturday morning, as the court was about to open, a telegram from New York, signed "E. R. Hill," was received, stating her inability to be present, and expressing her regrets.—*Springfield Union, Oct. 1st.*

NORTH BROOKFIELD.

Mrs. E. R. Hill's barn was destroyed by fire on Saturday evening. The trial of Mrs. E. R. Hill, which was to have taken place on Saturday, was postponed, as Mrs. Hill was unexpectedly called out of the State. Constable Bothwell, who held a warrant against her two days before she left town, depended upon her word to appear before the trial justice. Mrs. Hill is charged with mutilating valuable trees in Walnut Grove Cemetery. Putting the fire and the court cases together, the people of the town express the belief that the former was the result of an attempt to create sympathy for Mrs. Hill outside the town limits.—*Worcester Spy.*

Mrs. E. R. Hill is to be tried in Town Hall this morning at ten o'clock, before Justice Jenks, for mutilating trees in Walnut Grove Cemetery. Geo. F. Verry is for the prosecution.—*North Brookfield Journal, Sept. 29th.*

An outrageous piece of vandalism was committed at Walnut Grove Cemetery about a week ago, upon the lots of Rev. G. H. DeBevoise, Asahel Barlow and Mr. Doane. The limbs of trees on these were cut from the trunk to within a few feet of the top, on the side facing the lot of Mrs. E. R. Hill, on which she has just placed a monument. The trees are ruined as objects of beauty, and their growth in the future probably checked. Great indignation is felt in town, and all will be gratified to learn that the perpetrators will be brought to justice.—*North Brookfield Journal, Sept. 29th.*

These objects of beauty are the town's acknowledged nuisance.

Mrs. E. R. Hill's buildings were fired at 8 o'clock in the evening, thus having a torch light. Was it to pay for not having a court? There are more than fifty that ought to be examined by insurance agents. I demand they investigate that fire, set.

Mr. EDITOR:—We would like to inquire of the law-abiding and peace-loving citizens of North Brookfield, if it is not about time to put a veto upon such vandalism and abuse as has been carried on with a high hand in our town of late? I should say so, if there is any virtue in law and it be anything more than mere form. If a procession of mourning friends are to be hooted at and blackguarded as they carry their dead to his last repose, and even the cemetery, the place above all others we hold in reverent, tender regard, is to be desecrated in such a malicious manner, we believe it high time the perpetrators were brought to justice, and prevented from venting their malice any further.

X. Y. Z. et al.

—*North Brookfield Journal, Sept. 29th.*

Bloat, hitch on—Alpha and Omega—that is not enough, &c. You must not speak out loud and protect your own property from the above writer, who is going to take my last cent to build up his own false show. Did you tip over and smash those monuments in your haste to rush the building of the railroad through that sacred set-apart *Rest.* needlessly desp....g the same?

Rev. Mr. DeBevoise preached a timely and interesting sermon on the text, "We all do fade as a leaf," Sunday morning.—*North Brookfield Journal, Oct. 6th.*

Said DeBevoise looked awfully faded (more so than a leaf) on the Saturday morning before, with temper.

A telegram received from Mrs. Hill, Saturday, waiving an examination, put an end to the anticipations of the crowd ready to attend the trial, and now it seems very uncertain when it will come off. "A bird in the hand," &c.—*North Brookfield Journal, Oct.*

But you had the gathering at 8 P. M., torch light, &c.

The quiet of the town was disturbed about 8:30 P. M. last Saturday, by an alarm of fire caused by the burning of Mrs. E. R. Hill's barn. As the builing was small, and well filled with hay, the fire, by the time the engines arrived, had acquired such headway that it was impossible to extinguish the flames, and owing to the limited supply of water, all efforts were directed to save the house. As the premises have been unoccupied for the last week, the fire was doubtless the work of an incendiary. The loss is not half covered by insurance. The selectmen have taken the matter in hand promptly, and offer five hundred dollars reward for information that will lead to the conviction of the parties setting the fire.—*North Brookfield Journal, Oct.*

That means the reverse, reader, as my experience with said town can prove.

The insurance on the property destroyed is $165. The loss is nearer $1,500 than $1,000.

If some of those persons who are so loud and indignant in their condemnation of the despoilers of trees and shrubs in the cemetery would desist from walking over and standing upon graves and graded lots, they would evince much better tast and at the same time be more consistent.—*North Brookfield ournal.*

How about that mysterious axe, ladder, and saw?—*North Brookfield Journal, Oct. 13th.*

I bought and paid for the above mysterious implements in a hardware store in Brooklyn, and expected to be, or to have been, in a few days, at my own home, to have them in use, and not borrow in my hurrying, building, gathering fruit, &c. The ladders were stairs, and the latest issue, and expensive. But you keep me at bay. You want the whole to burn up. It was God's providence that the fire was squelched.

The witnesses in the case of the Commonwealth *vs.* Mrs. E. R. Hill, were before the Grand Jury, Tuesday.—*North Brookfield Journal, Oct 20th.*

What case is there before the Grand Jury? Is it the fiend's burning of my property?

Mrs. Hill has been heard from. Sheriff DeLand has received a telegram asking him to protect her house from the "fiendish and insatiable mob," and another inquiring if it was yet burned.—*North Brookfield Journal, Oct. 20th.*

Asking Insurance Agent Deland if my house was burned, *so that the contents were removed*, and requesting an anwer immediately. No reply.

October 25th.—At George P. Rowell & Co.'s I find a letter from North Brookfield. My heart leaps with joy to hear from a friend.

NORTH BROOKFIELD.

The selectmen have offered $500 reward for the conviction of the parties who set fire to Mrs. E. R. Hill's barn some time since, and there are lots of folks who think they know who did it. Mrs. Hill has disappeared and there is a general desire that she may be found, so that the public can know if the grand jury found an indictment against her.—*Spencer Sun, Oct. 19th.*

Grand Jury found an indictment for what?—for the fiends burning my building for a torch-light gathering?

Imagine, reader, for a moment my feelings on reading the above! Driven from my hard earned, little cosy home, among those with whom not one live being was found I had ever seen before, except through knowledge of books. My expenses more a day than has been my allowance per week at home. Aside from what my inheritance gave me, there is not a foot of land in my possession but that is teeming with sacred associations, *that is a society in memory's hall.* And to think those low minded reporters, banded together with the railroad masonic DeBevoise gang, which, on the evening after that, to be at DeBevoise's court, in their manaical disappointment at not having a chance to gloat, persecute, crush, and defame an upright, moral, *law-abiding*, lone, divorced, orphan, educated woman—burned my barn! But, reader, not alone in that little cottage where my loved children were born, sickened, and died! Every room, every corner and spot an association of those loved, lost, beautiful boys. That barn, with its many associations, besides the contents heretofore mentioned, had relics removed there not six weeks previous from a chamber in my house to give place for a black walnut chamber set bought of and delivered and set up by J. B. Lawrence & Co., Worcester, paying $110 for the same, and placing in said chamber a chestnut and black walnut set, bought of said Lawrence in 1865, paying for the same $65, that I have kept sacred, which were to be placed in this house and my L room, on completion; which would have been built wall around my mowings within the time I have been absent from my own, my native soil, and have comforts to make me comfortable in my old age. My lumber, doors with green glass lights, windows with four lights of glass, shingles, and every item for said building bargained for, and bill to be delivered from Forbush & Co. (and a lumber dealer next door), Worcester, cash on delivery. That money I had planned for the payment of the above is spent and over $200 more. My barn is burned and not one-tenth covered by insurance, to say nothing of those sacred relics that money, never, no, never could have bought ! And, reader, that barn was set on fire by those disappointed fiends who were gloating upon the farce of corruption of the law in the power of the ignorant and vicious. That will call forth such issues as the above notice seek to destroy truth and virtue, to cover their own sins and punishable crimes, and as Christ was a victim for similar causes, was no more innocent from them than am I to day, and as has heretofore been arraigned, belied, falsified in every way devisable, because I defend truth, law, justice, and mercy. And, reader, for the same I believe, from those vicious spirits the above alluded to gang, my life will be taken as Abraham Lincoln, John Bunyan, John Brown, Jesus Christ, and sundry others of the same type, come to a felon's end. Methinks I hear some of my my readers say : " How about that walnut DeBevoise tree." This is just how : " Those three valuable trees above alluded to are nearer seventy-five years old than fifty—they were my father's till within the last twenty years, and he sold a part of a walnut grove and pastures to the town—citizens and grave lot owners have long desired the removal of the walnut trees, because ruthless men wander upon graves gathering them and throwing sticks, clubs, and stones to bring the walnuts down. The fall of 1875, my children, in their new white water cemented bricked grave, with slate slab lid—some 2½ feet down upon top of which was basket, axe, and beetle bags, stones here and there upon said lot, where the boys had cracked them," &c.

The ladder on DeBevoise's lot against his tree which had been shaken. My lot seemed a chosen spot for their refuse, &c. Even the man DeBevoise kept more or less to keep his lot in good repair, would lay his truck, such as his sickle, jacket, basket, and often the fine grass would be placed on my monument stand, as well as the decayed flowers and toad stools, &c. Two boys also rolling on my sacred grave plot not two weeks before I left. I moved those implements, the boys went without assistance. I then and there thought could my dead boys live and have such beastly natures, I should have had reason to have wished them dead. Brewer and Perry had cut all of the walnut trees but those three,

Mr. Doane promising to cut his soon. Barlow—nobody had had a chance to tell him his tree was to be cut, though all knew he would be glad to have it down, DeBevoise resisting owing, without doubt, in part, it was thought, to keep his son from my and other people's lands.

Scores of times I have given James DeBevoise, when asked, permission to gather nuts gladly, for I had great influence over him when other teachers had failed. Many a time have school recitations been learned with alacrity, and committed to memory by my instruction and with the anticipation of getting bushels of walnuts. At the close of school we would hasten to my walnut grove, and those boys would shake and gather walnuts, not forgetting to crack and eat them, and rolling with laughter and jesting till the vaults of heaven would ring with their glee, and not one among them enjoyed it more than I; and those boys must remember the many times I have spoken against the walnut trees being left in the cemetery where graves were inhabited.

Elisha Perry told me as he was covering Homer R. Prouty's remains near my lot: "That they were going to cut those trees down; DeBevoise objects, but he will have to submit if you complain of them as a nuisance." I was telling him that my monument was to be erected the following Tuesday. It came Saturday A. M. before that time. I entered my complaint: the clubing and stoning of that tree—the other two are pig walnuts, not gathered. My lot sometimes was filled with stones, which had been thrown up to get those walnuts; this fall, the trees bearing well, and the branches filled were over my grave.

I told that committee of selectmen and the respectable citizens I could not nor would not permit such performance upon my darlings' graves. They all, every one of them, agreed with me, and said they ought and should be cut, the committee telling me to enter my written protest and complaint against the same, demanding them to be cut at once, as I suggested. Accordingly I wrote to DeBevoise, Doane, and Barlow, also grave yard committee, which has been heretofore printed.

The committee came not to my assistance, though being

specially sent for, as my monument was delivered. That committee knew well those boughs would have to come off; thus they staid back, ignominiously using me as an implement to bring about what they all wished done, but had not quite backbone enough to tell De Be. it should be done, though not one of them, as they have expressed to me heretofore, had a particle of ministerial respect for what I call the simple-minded, pugilistic earthy Gabriel. The young man who trimmed those branches had done the same upon trees in cemeteries in other places. Said young man cut the branches shorter than the law provides. Said point of law I never had investigated, though my walnut trees had been trimmed by graveyard committee in 1867. I have not noticed, but they are certainly cut upon my land with more of that trespass; also *telegraph wires and poles* have been removing branches with trespasser's sickle. Also railroad cut into trees out of the line, &c.

Reader, those walnut trees were not ornamental shrubs. They were a hideous nuisance to the sincere mourner and sensitive, refined, loving heart; (but to the coarse, the vicious who are ready to filch, and destroy character, gravestones, rob one of their land illegally, and defy humanity in every way thus. We have got the money, you have not, to bring a successful issue in court, as money rules, and not law and unimpeachable evidence). Since the war! Remember, reader, the different representations in the slips, the blackening calumny. The hideous falsification, purposely to tarnish my name if possible, and shall I not have the privilege to vindicate *my character thoroughly?* When money controls the newspapers—to publish the false representations—and not one line for me would those illegal railroad trespassing hordes permit on my part; nor even a lawyer is there. But the *cents* are closing their eyes. Some, many of those legal men are in the ditch of illegal advice, as report has it, and is evident by the evading and close; and let E. R. Hill bear the contumely of being arrested and imprisoned in a felon's cell, and other warrants, if I should break or cut one of the branches that grow over my land. Bothwell saying, "They don't hurt your land," &c. I can't have law and truth vindicated in North Brookfield, nor anywhere else, when the purse can buy men in authority. History has not upon record such open violation as I can prove in my railroad case—my false imprisonment case—the DeBevoise case for "mutilating valuable trees," &c. Oh, readers! stop, see those boys, men and women, throwing clubs and stones upon DeBevoise's walnut tree; they come down heavily on our darlings' grave. How many sticks and clubs there lie that have pelted them down, down in the grave; so low, mamma can't hear their wail; but she sees the clubs and stones are on darlings' grave and plot; those mortals, scared ("as with a red, hot iron"), now stand on darlings' grave, and jump up as they throw the club at the DeBevoise tree to get the walnuts the other side. Thus they are stamping darlings down! See the dripping upon grave-stones—a blackening stain, that cannot be removed. But, reader, see DeBevoise ready with his might to tarnish, to blacken my character, as you see he has already done, for a simple offence—an offence I would not permit to have been done had I known that line measure. But, thank God, it reveals Gabriel.

G. C. Lincoln and family moved into North Brookfield some fifteen years since. Said Lincoln, being fortunate in being Town Treasurer some seven or eight years, used the town's money, without paying interest, during said time. Very handy change for starting a grocery and dry goods business. Such handy change in time keeps one feeling strong. He gains wealth fast. He enlarges his phylacterie; builds and owns a nice house; buys his young and *promising* son a printing-press. They wax fat, and kick hot. The little son was horrified, as well as his father, at my writing DeBevoise the letter in this book. When I told the boy said letter should be published from pole to pole, the boy replied, "That would be mean," &c.

Lincoln has a son named Paul Gabriel DeBevoise Lincoln, as report has it. Paul's father is one of the selectmen that make the "town's indignation at the mutilation of those valuable trees," &c.

Does George Lincoln remember the times he and his sister and James DeBevoise have gathered walnuts in my grove, without permission as well as with? Stop and consider the false representations that small sheet has sent out. You have been weighed in the balance—and are found wanting. Selah.

But as it seems to have pleased some that I should thus be held a criminal as if guilty of a hideous crime, and DeBevoise catching at this straw of offense to aid the railroad Masonic thieves' false imprisonment, in their tumultuous iniquity, he rushes for judgment against me, forgetting entirely the passages "forgiven seventy times seven;" "if thy brother take thy coat, give him thy cloak also." If he strike upon the right cheek, turn the left for another crack! But the graveyard nuisance, the $175 monument, may be blackened—the little marker with Willie, Albert, little darlings Warren, Walter, and the mother's prayer on the other side of the little stone! "Tread softly! the ground is holy. See whose grave she weepeth o'er. Lo, the simple superscription: 'Little Darlings!'—nothing more." Methinks DeBevoise says "I'll blacken her character, and compel her to surrender her last dollar to us and our aggrandizement." Yes, Gabriel, you remind me of a narrow capacity tug-boat trying to tug iniquitous crafts to a shore. The smoke comes dense and dark from the small chimney. Why, those crafts are heavily laden, with dark, heavy coal weight—the black smoke is fanned by the breeze, and a spark is in that smoke. The wind wafts it to the barn. It blazes. Those crafts that the tug-boat has just got ashore are in one gang. Mrs. Hill we shall clean out to-night, root and branch. Oh, no; God is there in the presence of a few men. The engine must be worked. The flames are subdued. And, as if to carry out their fiendish longing, through every periodical they blaspheme my name. And, readers, how much sin was there in those branches being cut a little too short, compared with the sin of the abstracter of money, the horse-killer, the liar and hypocrite, so readily forgiven—if DeBevoise even thought they had sinned? Look at my crime. My name enrolled as it is above in items. This, reader, is the way I wish for truth to be vindicated. And my crime in having the monument men cut those limbs *too short* was through ignorance. But that ignorance shows conclusively what manner of spirit dwells in the breast of Gabriel DeBevoise. Heaven forbid his being permitted to preach long without investigation. Should it not be done, I can speak as a prophet that congregational piety will soon be numbered with the dead ologies. DeBevoise has never been the man to invite me to his church—my old home. And, readers, a scorpion's whips could not drive me into either church in North Brookfield till said churches 'bide the covenant obligations, which are used there when they will, as much as any horse jockey does his veracity. I will here, at this point, speak of a church discipline case. A. Smith, who was excommunicated under the ministry of Christopher Cushing, and Mr. Smith's own words to me, that more than a score of written sheets of foolscap paper, besides church meetings many and often, to try to get the wandering sheep back in the fold, all in vain. Thus years passed away, and Smith is still without the fold under discipline. Hurrah! the tug boat is going to land Smith in the harbor of the church. Smith gives $350 towards repairing the old church. The tug boat sends him clear in without one word, as report has it, from Howe and Whiting, but it's our duty to receive brother Smith in our new beginning, our dedication. Let us all dedicate our hearts anew to God, and you without sin throw the first stone. How does that compare with the walnut tree trimming too short. But there is another point here. Mrs. Hill must be subdued and not let that railroad proceeding have publicity. We must squelch her, lose no time, ere she makes publicity of our traffic. Put up the sails. We will outride her in this gale. Yes, reader, that is just the reason, and none other. The cause of my imprisonment—the cause of Gabriel's low, pugilistic, almost depraved treatment of me, the past year—to shield that crew that are supporting him. And I ask prayerfully, beseechingly, ought I not have this public way of vindicating my case through law, from which I rushed, telegraphing, as I did, in season, to Jenks, that morn of that fatal day. That savage powwow I nipped in the bud. I have told my fugitive tale from the moment I was one mile from my own house till I reached my abode in Brooklyn city. And I believe a Judas was not a hearer. My name to every one has been E. R. Hill. As much a fugitive from North Brookfield as any slave ever from southern domain, or Simms in Boston. To thwart this diabolical plot of citizens to prevent my being able to set forth the North Brookfield illegal proceedings in becoming an associate in building the North Brookfield railroad; also taking $6\frac{2}{3}$ per cent. of her valuation for the payment of the same. Their noncompliance with the statutes, in the taking of my land for railroad bed, their forbidding of my removing posts upon my land. They, those ring men, were ready to bind me hand and foot by calumny and poverty, strip me of my all. And, reader, this truth I send forth to vindicate the three issues pending in the courts at Worcester, where I cannot have the least show of chance with those masonic war officers. There is not a chance to stand against them, only by this truth being spread, and wise men from without to show to the world my justification in vindication of the statutes. If North Brookfield can sink their town into debt $6\frac{2}{3}$ per cent. of its valuation, become an associate corporation, rob people of their land as they will for their best party pockets, trampling under foot humanity, ignoring the statutes in divers ways—if it's North Brookfield's privilege to do this, why not every other town in the Union? Reader, I demand the statute laws to be enforced, and whoever tramples them under foot to be dealt with as their crime deserves — ever balancing with justice and mercy.

My book has, through necessity, been lengthened to one-third more than purposed, and my expenses also. I was home Sabbath day (4th November), at my cottage, for clothes and insurance papers, and a few tokens of the loved and lost. Oh, destruction! Oh, sin! Oh, my God! why oh, why, hast thou chosen me a battle-axe? Why driven

From the cot of my fathers; among strangers to dwell? cans't Thou, wilt Thou not bring good out of this evil? light out of this darkness? Thou who ridest amidst this storm. How bold they talk, and act! Perchance 'tis meet for them to treat me thus! "They demand my lip keep silence!!!" Thus I answer these dark coarse plots, with my pen's diamond point, tracing their awful doings—Thou God above canst make them retire abashed!

"Thy power is far more vast than finite mind can scan. Thy mercy is still greater shown to weak, dependant man."

Sabbath morn 8.30 A. M. I stepped out of the cars in that great "Union Depot," at Worcester. Out of it—off. How cold, frozen ground, ice spitting snow flakes! How dreary, as if all were frozen in the heart. I'll search for a soul that ain't frozen, that ain't seared as with a red hot iron to get money—who in their haste break down every obstacle that will retard their aspirations. They'll crush whether man, woman or child!!! Oh, God, keep me, this thy day from those maniac hounds—I turn this way and that, to get directions to a place I have been once before, where I know I left souls in God's image some weeks since.

I ring the bell—a familiar face—the door opens—a wide entrance. But oh! death has borne its suffering victim, who opened wide that door for me before (welcoming me in with God's blessing) to that bourne from whence no traveller returns! At breakfast table, where the utmost neatness, and style with abundance of nice and choice food, with sympathizing new found friends, giving to me, a stranger while my own town neighbors and confederates are stripping, robbing and driving me, helpless from my own hard earned and inherited sustenance with all the contumely they can heap on me to cover their own illegal sins, and diabolical shame. In going to the above place I pass a livery stable; there I'll apply for a carriage, driver, to convey me to what is left of the fiend's fire, my own house. We are off. How cold! before one mile the buffalo has to be wrapped tight about me, with fleet horse gliding along: the driver too is suffering with cold. But the steed is hurried on. Ere we reach the village I think it best to stop at a farmer's residence where beast and man can be provided for, &c.

The chill has done its work, but I must not submit to its effects; I goad myself on for the nearing scene. We are there. The driver reins his horse, and waits.

That warm young Irish heart, speak not, moves not, till he is asked. I was surprised—the windows and doors and roof of my house remained unburnt. Oh that DeBevoise court disappointment was "robbed by God's special interposition of part of its torchlight jubilee they meant (as Bothwell told me in the cell) to clear everything out that would be a reminder. The man meant to get my last dollar. But rea ler, my great work will live as long as the Bible, and my persecution as John Brown's, John Bunyan's and many others.

I cannot—cannot attempt this winter to face that ruin, and if satan himself had been divested of his every attribute and his mantle had fallen upon a few making themselves notable by illegal traffic, who hates the sight of one who will not join, or countenance their bastard estate, and glory, I am thus compelled by them to kiss this token, this sacred spot, gather a few things to protect me from the cold, and ere I get my trunk half filled my door bell rings. I say, please go to the other door. As I pass along, I see, oh, horror! the fiend of fiends, that false imp Sylvander Bothwell. Young man, rush and lock that door, don't you let that devil enter. That's the fiend who assailed me, on my own land without cause, without warrant, thrust me in a felon's cell to gloat his own and others' malicious design, I ordered him from my premises. He stays, walks here and there, making mock of me, a woman who never violated a statute law (only my monument man cut that old walnut tree *limbs too short*)! and that lying whelp of sin, that trespassing devil hanging round me; there is not a convict in prison on God's footstool that deserves that sentence more than the above Bothwell. His name defiles the page I write. Is there no law to keep that trespasser on my premises? I demand him to leave. He with dripping glands says, "you stop, or I'll arrest you." Reader, can I not go in to my own house, and order this or any other trespasser from my premises Sabbath day, without the threat of arrest? The young man passes out. The trespasser says to the young man "She's crazy as she can be, she ought to be in the hospital." Yes, reader, my telling that man to leave,—I forbade his touching or stepping upon my premises—would have put me in the Insane Hospital; I should been manacled off. That's the state of mind, that the illegal proceeding of the railroad iniquity of different dyes have sunk North Brookfield in. To be hindered thus, I cannot call to Mr. Haston to my father's house, to babies' grave. Oh God, come quick with they scythe of justice. Strengthen me, Oh God, in the power of thy might to conquer that den of iniquity, that marplot of corruption under the banner of christianity. Let them commune and go away from that communion to crucify their Lord. As the above man came from that "set apart blood" to goad me in my own house, that man had my house key during the night of my incarcaration in the felon's cell—my drawer was robbed of $70, and that was the most trivial offence against me that took place during the twenty hours' incarceration. Do you think that man's hand is to be placed upon my shoulder at every flash of his ungovernable illiterate temper? I ask and demand, as a law abiding truthful female citizen, the protection of the United States Court, to keep from harm my person, my property, from those who are vested in legal authority in North Brookfield, Massachusetts, who have violated and outraged and trespassed the statutes of Massachusetts of decency, of humanity! I am not "Simms" "nor one of old Legree slaves," "nor Ginx's Baby." But a lady or female or a woman somewhat educated; my father was not moving from "Dan to Beersheba"; but owned that great farm house and the one hundred and eighty acres of land connected with it, with fruit of every variety in our youthful days, and the forests of walnut and chestnut. The hundreds of rock maples—oh those sugar hours! We children had all that earth could give, and those poor menials that have come in from other States, "had shelter and board in that house without pay, but your welcome boys, do the best you can." Some of those recipients are hounding me to-day. Methinks I hear my readers saying. "Why, she condemns the town *en masse*." Reader, how can I speak otherwise? The three selectmen are masons; they are all located within thirty rods of the felons' cell. That man spoken of before, has thrust men into the cell in his madman temper, but they were released in less than an hour, but an educated, law-abiding self-respecting person at all times, and in all places a public educator, a newspaper reporter, can be thrust into a felons' cell, because she said upon her own land a gamblers' funeral horse cannot be hitched to my bars. I untied the tie rein; I did not move a horse, I did not speak above my usual tone only when calling to the next bars, and that, in voice for the distance required, and *no higher*. The disturbance was Bothwell's shouts, seizing me and throwing me down on my own land, and carrying me off my own property as a beast, and thrusting me in a felons' cell. The second time his vile hands have defiled my physical frame, and agonized my sensitive nature. He still continues to prowl and trespass upon my land; for every time of illegal outrage and trespass I demand a legal hearing. I was driven from Masachusetts for protection in this hour of peril; and Almighty God above guided the fugitive E R. Hill to this harbor. Thus the appeal from Jenks and Bothwell, is to be met in the Superior Court. My waving the DeBevoise nuisance—"old walnut trees cut to short branches"; is to have hearing. I did not utter one word to Bothwell, when he told me he had a warrant for my arrest, and another all ready, if I cut a bough from a tree hanging over my land. I did not make a sound, no more than Christ did, in a similar time. The reason given for his not speaking, is, "that we might have an all prevailing plea"; the reason I did not speak, was, I was before given into the power of that Bothwell, and I knew enough not to speak, knowing the devil was desirous to have me, "that he might sift me as wheat;" and God was permitting, &c. How about, run away, to telegraph, as the dispatches sent, inform the readers. Behold, the black, lying scandal those newspaper items gull out! North Brookfield sent news, that, they meant to brand me, call a court, and have their own lawyer, without one word on my part. Reader, see how cut and dried! As J. Duncan used my name maliciously to cover over an error, even so with the **North Brookfield Railroad Corporation. They don't want their** fearful violation of the statutes to be made public, and, as I am the only mortal woman outside of the rings in that town who can report and can tell coherently what has been said in public meetings, &c., this makes me a dangerous person, like those spoken of in the Bible. A heavy lawsuit was to be brought, forbidding that illegal railroad debt to be paid out of the tax-payers' purses, but letting the directors pay for their own monstrosity, that was making them so *great* and *rich*. I have more reason to pay homage and respect to the Northampton bank robbers than to the North Brookfield Railroad men. That railroad proceeding, if left unchecked and unrebuked, would, or is enough to, bring ruin upon any town in the State in the Union, and were it to be so left unrebuked it would be far worse than bank robbery. I did not pay my tax under protest to get back *that dollar*. That is the handle, reader, to the key that unlocks the bolt, and that will bring investigation of that $6\frac{2}{3}$ cents tax on North Brookfield valuation, and its becoming an associate.

I have got to have a lawyer out of Worcester County. Report has it there are some—oh, what is it? Advice is not always cheap, and if you pay dearly for legal advice, it may be so shallow that one will pay more dearly by following the said advice than for the counsel fee—at least, that has been my experience with attorneys, where that great depot is, since the war. I asked Geo. F. Hoar, my old counsel, to aid me in law after my incarceration in the felons' cell on the 22d of September (said Hoar being only from August to December older than myself, as he has told me heretofore). Hoar imperatively refused, adding that he must be at Washington on the 15th, &c. "Yes, but I thought as you knew me, and had some experience in the Stoddard and W. Railroad court," &c. Hoar: "Mrs. Hill, I should not have entered into that case at all had I not been given to understand and been assured that it would have been settled without trial," &c. Mr. Hoar was the third different lawyer employed on said case, some of Stoddard and Whiting's other counsel proving to be masons, and so on. I will here say that Hoar's partner is counsel for the town, &c. Whiting has told me that " the town's counsel was thoroughly disgusted with their proceedings." Reader, I had no more thought of having Hoar for counsel than, &c., knowing the circumstances, I asked him, and took witness purposely to have the refusal. Hoar is a woman suffragist; *I am not.* Neither am I a politician. But Hoar's vote at Washington last fall made *me see, and I understand* how things work, since the war and woman suffrage *promulgation.*

I asked an Irish lawyer the same day to look up the Nye trespass, but he did not want part of the job, &c.; I also asked a promising young lawyer to take my case, sincerely desiring him as an advocate; and I believe he desired also to obtain justice in every case of mine at issue, and he accepted. The next morning he said his business was going to be so great that he could not undertake my case, but was desirous of a successful issue for me, which he knew must come. Reader, that man had to face a boughten crew, whose doings I believe in his heart he scorned as he would the bottomless pit. Thus, you see, I saw at once his predicament. I said then, and there to him that I should never attempt to go into court in Worcester City until there were new officials—not of the war type, or masons. I wish to bring in a few more incidents of recent date.

At my mother's death her thirds, &c., were to be divided. Hon. Wm. Mixter, Hon. Chs. Adams, Jr., and a gentleman from Spencer (his name is gone from me) were legally appointed for said purpose. Said division was disappointing to my eldest brother at the homestead, said parties not giving him what he asked for, and what outsiders, even, thought ought to have been his special portion. That notable era was on Saturday, May 27, 1867, appointed for my accommodation, as I was teaching on Ragged Hill, West Brookfield, eight miles off.

My brother was stirred to the very citadel of his being at the said partition. Thus, as I lie on my couch at my own little cozy home, I turned this way, that, and the other, I thought and thought how I might get that house and yard, &c., into my said brother's possession. Accordingly, next morning I called on Mrs. Wm. Beecher, before alluded to, telling her, that Sabbath morn, my anxiety and desire. Calling on God to bless our every word, Mrs. Beecher said: "Mrs. Hill, your great heart is to help, to rescue, let what will betide. Your undertaking is a mountainous job, &c. If you can buy the doctor out, &c., as you suggest, I will loan you money if the doctor wants money instead of your note. I must laugh at your noble peradventures; I'll trust you with my money without security," &c. Off I went to see and tell Mrs. Lane. Mrs. Lane said: "Oh, my dear child, I can't, I can't advise you, to; your heart and purpose are good, are noble, but I fear, I can't advise you, to, because of their previous doings." " Oh, my faithful guide! have we not, is it not, in this time, if I can, a duty, a need, for my said brother (drop the past) to get for him, if I can, the possession of said house and surroundings. The doctor has a good house, &c.; my sister also, and I, my little cot. How different it will ring for my brother in need to say, 'I own this house—our father's house.'" Mrs. Lane: "I could not undertake what you suggest on any consideration. I see plainly you are determined to undertake the matter, and talk will be vain. I will pray God to guide you, keep you as the apple of His eye." At the homestead—my brother at his table; his face covered with his hands—" Good morning —blue? Come, I am in for a rescue this holy day. This "plucking of corn on the Sabbath," "the sheep in the ditch," &c. Now for a hearing: "Brother, will you give me so much for my share and the doctor's (if I can buy it of him); pay me $100 down; give me as security for the remainder a mortgage on all your real estate at this homestead (also pledging, when you wish, that you will give me first chance to buy, &c.) for security on the remaining sum." My brother leaped with exultation at this unexpected ray of hope in his gloom. " Yes, I will gladly; I can give you the $100 bill (showing it) this instant. But the doctor won't sell to you if he should mistrust you and suspect that you thought of selling to me. Mrs. Stoddard means to come here. Warren will sell to her, and not to you. Let that part rest." "You pledge solemnly the above?" "Yes; take the $100 bill as a bond." "No, not to-day. To-morrow morning I will take your gig and pacer; drive over to Ragged Hill; teach my school, and return here after school in the afternoon. Then I will go direct to the doctor's office, and strike a trade, if possible, and buy his share, trusting, in God's own time, again to live in this, my father's house. I'm going to church this afternoon. Rest in peace till I see you again. Good morning." I did attend church in the afternoon, and third service also. Monday, 29th, 7 A. M., I was wending my way in a gig (pride in pocket; also $100) to my school-room—a wide-awake school that. I got home in the afternoon. At the doctor's office—Doctor: " Hallo! where do you come from?" " Ragged Hill." Doctor : " Been in school to-day?" " Yes." Doctor : " Mighty, what's up ?" " That's just the question. I want to buy your share ; so and so will give so much." Doctor: " You may have it. I had much rather cut off coupons than till land," &c. " I have not money enough to give you all ; here's $100 ; this bank book I will make over to you ; the remainder I shall have to borrow if you will not take my note." Doctor : " I'd just as soon have your note ; we will go this minute down to Nye's (not 10 rods off) and have the deed made at once." At Nye's the deed was made out complete, the doctor's wife signing. we went off each to our own abode. Ere I reached mine, I met the waiting brother. With quick step we entered Nye's. Said Nye was surprised to a marvel, and said "Mr. Tyler, your sister is doing a great thing. Why, this sudden, all unexpected move is making (in putting together again this property), you worth more by $1,000." My brother shed tears of joy, saying, " I know what she is doing; the other two would not have helped me to a 'red.'" "What a woman you are," says Nye, laughing and writing the deed and mortgage. The clock struck eleven just as we rose to leave. I did not read my mortgage. I had no thought of a mistake. In the morning I left the same under seal with Mrs. Beecher. She smilingly says, "you heroine," &c. The next morning my brother with his fiery steed takes me and leaves me at Ragged Hill school-house. Next time at home Nye tells me of my sister coming to him in great wrath about the above proceeding. The doctor, feeling sorry, supposed I was going to keep it myself, &c. Nye adding, that day alone was your success. (That sister's son is just so yet.) In December, 1874, owing to misfortune, my brother was unable to meet my payments or pay interest. I was willing all should remain, wishing him to have the mortgage and note acknowledge interest on interest, as I had been sick—not earning for nearly two years. The Duncan slander had cost heavily (by having counsel of R. Beecher and the Bartlett recommendation). I was needing money when at Worcester. My brother told me to have that mortgage made as I desired, giving me writing for its security. Bacon was not at his office. Knowing J. Henry Hill, I showed him said mortgage. He said the mortgage was only on an undivided portion of my mother's thirds. According to my statement, I was not secured for one-third of the dues. I was astounded. Reader, I never had read that mortgage. I went back to P. C. Bacon's office. He tells me the same; sends me to the Probate Court-house for records of the divided thirds made by before-mentioned gentlemen, which I had bought and sold specifically. Stevens and Clerk searched a full day in vain; they seeing the court appointment for said division. At last Mr. Stevens and Bacon told me to go home to Nye, and get the papers. I went. Nye was confused; knew nothing about it now, and he should not think anything about it! "You won't? I guess Peter C. Bacon can make you think, as that gentleman sent me here for the same." Nye—"Did Bacon send for the papers?" "He did, sir. The divisions I have paid for, &c., must be defined in record without delay. Your blunder, or ignorance, has placed me in financial ruin, if the parties concerned should act a thousandth part as mean as you have." Nye searched here and there. He knew the divisions—how I bought and sold. Mixter is dead. "If the doctor had the mortgage on the homestead, as you have, it would not be necessary to find the papers." "Sir, it's my mortgage, and 'tis necessary." "I will look in the morning, and come to your house with information."

The next day he takes Dr. Tyler to Worcester, to P. C. Bacon, and said the parties thus agreed. A fearful fabrication of his own. Bacon knew it. Bacon made him

measure the bounds of land. I had bought and paid for
the half, house, &c.; and Bacon, in December, 1874, made
the conveyance. Reader, you ought to have seen that little
bantam Nye out with his compass, measuring land in the
freezing cold. The bantam urged said brother to let the
doctor have the mortgage and pay me up, as I wanted
the money so much. The transfer was negotiated then and
there, Bacon thinking the money better for me. Oh, oh, oh!
Bacon, how little you can know what it is to be in somebody
else's place. The doctor has now his long desire, and I
wronged most fearfully! B. Nye has stopped not in his
every move to take everything he can get in his pig-eye
aspirations upon mine for his and a few others' emolument.
Reader, see that eighty-year-old sending Scotchmen, Italians
and Irishmen upon my land, to get stones I have piled for
my own use, to fill up and bridge up the railroad bed,
&c. The remainder hereafter. Reader, look at A. Smith
again—why his way, and none other. His store seems like
a dice-box. Your eye would be weary to see how often his
mortgage deeds are advertised. Step into his store a minute.
His head a peck measure might encase. His hair being
like the negro, only grey, with great abundance. He has
very social, attractive ways—laying one hand into the other
inside up, sort of a move, with a phthisicky cough, standing
between counters to greet the comers in. "Walk into my
parlor, said the spider to the fly." Oh, you illiterate man,
soon the mortgage sells you out. How the greeting to-
day? Ben Dean is off, moving buildings. He leaves $100
with his wife, to pay to said Smith on account. She leaves
it, comes direct to my house with her oldest daughter that
I have been fitting for a teacher. She tells me of paying
that $100 that morning. Smith, in his hurry, don't make
minute of it, and a long, tedious law-suit is the consequence,
costing both a number of hundred dollars. The tax-bills
speak loudly of his wealth. He is the man who told me to
sit down in town meeting, when I whisperingly asked him
to count the vote, instead of yea and nay, because of the
illegal votes. "I tell you sit down, or an officer will come
and put this woman out of the hall." Reader, remember I did

not go in or out that hall without Cons. Lombard. When Lombard and I were in the ante-room he said he saw the boys and others vote, and he had seen it many times before. "But, oh, Mrs. Hill, you see how they feel towards you—don't, for God's sake and mine!" Didn't I dig for parts unknown till he cooled off. Then, to see that "dice-box" on my land, to appraise it! J. E. Porter, that can't influence, because he don't want to, that brother-in-law, double distilled, to pay for my hay, that horse ate, that drew the coal, that lay in house Barlow built, who owns one of those trimmed walnuts. And I ain't afraid to guess that Barlow will prove to have a soul of dimensions.

J. E. Porter sold some building lots from said Barlow lot at a fabulous price, and then called on the town to lay out a road before said house-lots, and demurred that he did not have three times allowed him for land for said road, though said road was enhancing the value of his estate thousands. That man appraising my land that is cut in that fearful way, as the profile tells the reader. See him and Gabriel at a Chicago Christian gathering—so pious, so ready to do good in the vineyard of the Lord. Reader, let me here take you to the Genett farm, where Sandy-flash steals from one to give to another. Both forgetting, of course, that a sister in Christ they have left behind out of the fold in North Brookfield, without one call to get her in the fold again; but we will strip her fleece all off clean, send her naked bleating into the cold world. And we'll have to help spread the Gospel with what we can get from her fleece, &c. DeBevoise, &c., God is not mocked. Your prayers there were as sounding brass and tinkling cymbals at Chicago—right from North Brookfield, Mass., not your native land, *but mine*, from which I have been driven, to find shelter from the fleecers and wolves. And the three last-named, are they not co-workers in the illegal traffic set forth in this book? That I cry in agony of soul for help, for guidance in my need, in a stranger's home!

Reader, back to November 4th. I hustled a few things more into my trunk, the driver doing the most. Thus was I robbed of a few hours'—in my house of mourning peace by Bothwell, the trespasser. No hell was ever described that could give him justice. The next morning, at Worcester, when arranging my trunk, the driver rings the bell, and leaves my four babies' locket—my small amount of jewelry, that I was just trying to think where I laid them, when Bothwell met my gaze on my forbidden ground.

Not having my policy, and having my mail sent from North Brookfield, November 2d, in which was a letter from the insurance company dated October 4th, saying my policy would cease the 24th, M. My premium and policy I own, expires April 1st, M., 1881. Luther Deland, agent, the telegraphed in this book you remember, &c. On said letter read, in print, if not taken out in ten days, return to said office. Saturday eve'g, Nov. 3d, 4.30 P.M., I take the steamboat for W. Nov. 5, I enter, present myself—and such audacity—the blood mounts high as I write. Sum it up thus : " We will pay the insurance on the barn, as you are a great loser, after we hold a meeting, Wednesday next, but we can't protect your house, if it is vacant," &c., " any longer." " Gentlemen, when I left my house, I expected to return to the same in less than two weeks, my health and other circumstances connected with the book to be soon issued prevented." On the 13th of October, 5 P.M., I heard of my loss; it crushed me again to hear ; omnipotent and omniscient power alone sustained me. I tried in vain to hear from Luther Deland. I will here relate an incident. In 1850 (something), Mr. Hill had bought part of a nice beef filling a barrel with choice roasts, steak, and so on, setting said barrel above the well, against a five foot embankment, to freeze. One morning, with his lantern, he went to said barrel for steak for the family breakfast. When, lo! the barrel was tipped over empty. A thief, not two legged but four, had been there. A roast bone— he looks farther—he sees fresh mounds here and there, he digs up one, it's his meat. A dozen would not count the new "dog graves." He comes in by being called —" Is that steak coming for breakfast?" The proprietor enters with a gnawed roast, hands it to me with a mad dismay—" It's the best I can get this morning." A loud ha, ha! came from my empty shell, the combination scene just made. Lloydy saying, hurriedly, " Grandpa's dog did not do that, papa, I know, it was some starved cur, wasn't it, papa?" "Yes; some poor cuss that keeps a dog half fed," &c. The dog's coming was watched for; before noon he came round, took a cursory view of his new market field and proceeded to uncover, pawed out a chunk heavy as himself, to all appearances, and marched off boldly, cross lots and other ways, Mr. Hill following in the distance. The dog brought up at Chauncy Edmunds' cottage house where Luther Deland lived, in quite small, close apartments. Thus his dog had a good sumptuous store filled with stolen meat for future need. It wasn't paid for. No, that was carelessness, like leaving my watch, 1875, on the recitation table since, &c. I told Mr. Hill then, when the dog proceeding which was a type and shadow of something to come, should be fulfilled, I hoped to be able to understand the riddle. Mr. Hill thought the barrel of meat returned to him would be the understanding for him. Reader, how about this insurance policy, why is Deland so still and silent, when in agony of soul I telegraphed him to take in his special custody my house and all therein from those, or that unsatiated mob. He has of late been with DeBevoise. Is DeBevoise tugging him, too? Luther Deland and wife left the old church and went to the Union when DeBevoise first came to North Brookfield. That lost r in DeBevoise's pronounciation was more than they could endure, &c. I will just say I liked DeBevoise's sermons first so much, I did not miss the r. I have not been able not to miss it of late. For instance, when he says in school, " Childwin it is a gweat thing to have yow name enwolled in pwint."

As to my house being unoccupied, it has been vacant by my absence from the same twelve weeks at a time teaching—four, five, six, eight, ten weeks, a common thing. And never before as now left unoccupied with the uninsured value, my income, my all. And the vandals have driven me from my own home. Their name ought to be the serpent's walking as the Bible tells about instead of crawling.

The insurance agent said he would recommend me to go next door or somewhere. " Sir, your deal does not meet my comprehension, you wish to put off your insurance blanket

—leave my house unprotected against the mob in North Brookfield, which it is your duty to investigate and bring the culprits to justice. But your agent there is not tending to business as he did in the Duncan's fire," &c. "What meaneth it?" I see, sir, what it means. The rabble want to destroy the rest and not have me get one cent. That is the cut and dried plan. My house has double the value in it that it had when insured. My barn and contents not one tenth insured. My farm income is all gone, the labor is paid for that had done the hard labor. I demand you, as recipient of my premiums and policies paid you, that you take charge of said property, from which 1 am driven for safety to my life and character." The rest I leave for a future time.

You cannot fail to see the hang together of the nests to destroy whoever questions their right to take rough shod, whatever they wish. My wood in small piles here and there, if not stolen, those walnut tree butts as fallen. My L not built, my barn gone, and my many well directed plans defeated, driven out from my house among strangers. And with fiendish glut they are reaching for the last penny. The Norway spruce about my tomb, just as they were felled, if they had been left standing, Mr. Sampson's barn and house must have been burnt. The money all used up. That those repairs and additions would have been made had it not been for the satanic designs and acts that came of the North Brookfield Railroad, whose treacherous illegality cannot be equalled in history. I appeal again to every man and woman to aid in showing up the false glitter of those men rushing themselves into notoriety on illgotten gains.

I ought to have related an incident which took place March 28 or 29th, 1871. The day after that Duncan notice I was at Hartford, Connecticut, at Catherine Beecher's Seminary, where I was expected as a teacher. On reaching said seminary, I found that the week previous Miss Catherine Beecher had transferred said position to a niece, Miss Mary Beecher, thus that prospect was at an end. Miss Beecher urged me to spend the night with them, but desiring to learn some facts connected with Duncan, &c., stopped at the Allyn

House. I was a guest at the Allyn House, Hartford, where my name can be found registered. During my stay in said hotel Augustus Smith and daughter and some others, saw me, between the hours of twelve and one, midnight, walking insanely about J. Duncan's premises; it was heralded from Dan to Beersheba, for the benefit of Jim and family, to cover their sins. After the prairie fire slander spread, it was told by Robert Beecher much to my chagrin; I was certainly in Hartford, Connecticut, that night, and he could not for his life see how I could be in North Brookfield. Jim and Augustus, finding that would not work out, Jim drove round, saying it was his maid out listening to the band in the town hall His maid's figure is as much like mine as an elephant is like an antelope, nevertheless, reader, that is the goggles and brain of North Brookfield, when they wish to start a "high" of their peculiar caste. And never in my life did I ever step or encroach, out of season, or out of place, upon a spot, place or thing. My uprightness is unimpeachable. The falsifications of that marplot of iniquity alleged to my name are their own monstrosities by birth, and upon their own shoulders at last "roost."

NOVEMBER 3D, 1877.

NORTH BROOKFIELD JOURNAL NEWS.

"Mrs. E. R. Hill shortly issues a pamphlet containing an account of her wrongs."

NOVEMBER 10TH.

"Mrs. E. R. Hill was in town last Sunday."

"Mrs. E. R. Hill was in town Sunday. She is writing a book, shortly to be published, which will give the author's opinions concerning 'matters and things' which have transpired in this town during the past twenty years or so."

I was home said Sunday; just hoping I could see my ruins, get some clothes to wear, get baby's hair, and insurance policy, and some money I.had written for to one who would not have (nor never before when asked) refused, had it not been for this crucifixion hour! I came home alone as soon as I could venture with health sufficient to meet the sight you had made and the destruction of my hard earnings. There were many choice, sacred, useful, necessary articles in that barn, having placed them there till that room was built. Had you come and tendered me $500 for those specific articles, I should have said: "Go! beggarly stone hearts; go your way!"—That $500 is not included in my estimate. The town has offered $500 reward. To me it seems the public's farce to cover that sin—will it be uncovered if they can help it, like the Jas. Duncan case?

"We'll clear Mrs. Hill out; she will have no money to rebuild." Another incident right here: My man, Robert Morse, after that felon court, was fairly beset, to his disgust and indignation, while waiting with carriage at the Town Hall during that farce court. "Great style, eh?" "Where does Mrs. Hill get her money?" "Hurrah for style!" "Who foots the bill?" &c., &c., from old heads and young. After his day's work, Tim Clark, Alf. Bartlett, and other "Cheap freight!" railroad men, would hail him thus: "Does Mrs. Hill pay you?" "Where does she get her money?" &c.

Many others asked that man the same impudent questions. It seems to me to have been their preparatory arrangement to clean my buildings out, and be certain I had no place to live, and no money to meet my cases in court! One paper issued some one outside "burnt the barn to get up sympathy." How transparent a subterfuge, to try to cover that guilt! What sympathy is going to give me my lost, lost property? Oh, you fiends of sin! Await your doom! God's time, not mine!

As Morse was driving home from Mrs. Ayres' rowan mowing lot, Bothwell walks in front of the span, saying, "Morse, did you cut those branches for Mrs. Hill?" "I did not." "Who did?" "You can ask Mrs. Hill." The whip cracks, the span start and so does B.!

In crossing and recrossing the East River, while overhead the rolling wheels stretches from column to column the cable, that is now spanning the river, and the boat crowded with passengers, at all times of day, I always press to the forward part of the boat, that I may see and learn what men cannot convey with the tongue. The thoughts that crowd into my brain in this "harvest time" would fill a volume. Oh, young man (just stepping outside the chain), a step more, and you would go down, down into that leaden water—while the leaden sky overhead would seem that not one ray of hope could be sent for your rescue. Not so with my brother—whom you look so much like—the water he stepped into, with seven others, was clear and transparent. The sun shone bright on that June afternoon. Everything was as clear and bright as the day star on high. That step of that loved brother put on his immortality the 28th of June, 1854. I am on a sick-bed in that very house—with a baby eighteen days old I am fugitive from to-day. John Hill, with my husband, comes to my bedside—they take my hands: "Elizabeth, keep calm, keep calm, for Albert is no more! He was drowned about two o'clock while bathing with Doctor ——— and Lawyer ———, and others." Peace! 'tis the Lord Jehovah's hand that blasts our joys in death! Midnight, and that beautiful, manly, lifeless form is in father's parlor, not forty-eight hours since he crossed the same threshold full of life and soul. June 30th the town is *en masse*, as with solemn tread they bear that noble youth of twenty years to his dry grave. They halt in front of the Hill cottage; a table is placed beneath the front window; the casket is taken from the hearse and placed on the table, for his sister, Mrs. Hill, is wrapped up, in the old arm-chair, at that window; the lid is removed, and that red-cheeked brother lays as if asleep, just ready to smile. Oh, Death! thou hast the fairest of the flock!

July 4th, 1854—midnight. I am dreaming. A fearful hailstorm pelting the windows as if they must crush them. I awaken, my eyes open; the room, with its white curtains, is as light as fire could make it. I shriek. The house is in flames! "Mr. Hill—Lloyd—we are on fire!—the house is on fire!" My nurse, with the babe in her arms, gets off my bed in bewilderment; she moves here and there senseless. I get off the bed, and with maniacal strength open wide the outside door, and screech, "Fire! fire!" I see that the old

Dana meeting-house is one blaze. Lloyd is pulling me back. "Mother, you'll die! you'll die! Come in till we can get you out! Do, mother, do!" The cinders and sparks have set our house on fire; our windows are cracking; my bed blanket, on the footboard of my bed, has caught; I grasp it with a hymn book on the carpet I put the fire out, and wrap the blanket about me, (that blanket is still in that house if it has not been stolen); in my sick-robe and slippers, and the blanket; Lloyd leads me out, his little arms around as far as he could reach, my limbs reeling me like a drunken man· he lays me down under an apple-tree, away from cinders and sparks, runs back and brings pillows and blankets, leaving me upon them, and with kisses said "Don't die, mama, don't die!" "Lloyd, God will keep me." "I'll go and carry that Bible (a large beautiful Bible I gave him as his seventh year's birthday present) on to grandpa's mowing, every-. thing else as fast as I can. Rest and live, mama." That noble boy is ten years old (the one that weighed three and a quarter pounds all dressed). He would rush to me every time he came back from grandpa's mowing, looking, off! Once he stopped; "Papa has fainted; they have brought him too. I told him to sit still on his trunk; he can't do a thing. He's as white as you are, mamma. A pretty time to faint, ain't it, mamma?" With a kiss he bounds off, soon reappearing with some men and a door. They place the door on rails, with bed, and thus I am laid on the door and carried by six men into Mr. Lewis Whiting's house. I did not speak, nor could not till the following afternoon; I knew, but could not speak. After sleep, when waking, I called for my baby. Llody, kissing me : " I'll bring brother from Mr. Fullum's as soon as they will let me—he is asleep and well, mamma. The house ain't burnt up, only the windows, and the carpets under the windows, the roof and not much ; oh mama, rest, sleep, do." That precious, faithful, loving son; that was beyond his years in every way; he could tell the texts, different parts of sermons with accuracy. The winter he was four years old, in school, Dr. Snell (committee) visiting the school, in talking to the scholars, wanted to know if there was a boy or girl in the school that could repeat the Fourth Commandment, to rise and repeat it. No one seemed to know anything about it; Llody, in one of the lowest seats rises and repeats the Fourth Commandment word for word, and sits down. Dr. Snell was affected to tears—" Llody you are a promising boy, God bless you; children, Lloyd's mother instructs him and guides him, and the seed there sown will spring up into everlasting life; let us pray." Dr. Snell, Dr. Cushing, Rev. Wm. Beecher,—all were faithful in the promised charge over me and my household. DeBe. has not been at my door but once, since his wife's death, and then there to ask me to contribute towards graveling the walk around his grave plot, as one side was my walk. I attempted to speak at that time of the desecration of graves, in the picking of walnuts, &c.; he walks right off without the least notice, "Briefly, I will let you know as soon as I can what your amount to pay will be." I was perfectly disgusted with him that moment. "You want my money and that is all you care for; my soul, or the dead bodies of my children is of no account." I have been at babies' grave and he came to his plot with somebody. I see enough, and I certainly hope and pray God's time will remove DeBevoise, so that his remains will not ever lie by my dead children, and where my right is to be laid in brick vault when *killed* by the mob! I have said, and will pen here. I hope DeBevoise will be buried on his native land, if such place can be found, for such a pugilistic spirit as he possesses must have a great amount of *phosphorus in his carcass* enough *perhaps* to set the very *earth* on fire, and thus commence that great read about day! Thus the very earth through DeBevoise will burn mine, and me first.

I wish to speak of my little cottage-home, subject to another incident. In spring time of 1868, during vacation, I had been at Worcester spending some days (in said city where I have purchased for the last twenty years $\frac{99}{100}$ of my necessaries, not including *groceries*. The day after returning home on one of those tours, after performing my daily round at home, after ablution—on my sofa for rest,—a strong smoke scent came into my room. I up, and pulled the curtain, east. The smoke is rising around my *tomb*. I rush below, take a pail of water, broom, screeching, fire, fire. Daguerrian Cary is burning raspberry-bushes and brush. One of the most windy days of spring; the flames leave that pile and rush on to my territory within three feet of my tomb, and that simple man back of the flames striking to put out the running fire. I shout, "for God's sake, come here and don't let it reach these fir trees over my dead boys." The neighbors rush with brooms and shovels; and when subdued, I said to Cary, "how came this fire?" "Cary was burning brush, &c." "Burning brush such a windy day as this?" Cary: "Yes, burning brush such a windy day as this." A man that knows no more than to do that, ought to have a guardian!" That killed me, Cary will hunt me down till he dies for this truthful suggestion. Had I not been home that day no power could have saved my buildings because of the Norway Spruce trees.

Thus I have been set on fire: First, on the northwest side; second, on the southeast side; third, on the south side, nine feet from my dwelling-house—the distance between the house and barn. Reader, you must see their next flank movement must be north of the house. The insurance company, whose policy I have in my possession, did their best to uncover that house—throwing it unprotected into that savage mob's power, which, I feel in my inmost soul, they long to bring to the same ashes as the barn. I have not a red cent to cover the loss. That their purpose and design to ruin me is rampant, is apparent as noon day. See, right from the communion comes trespassing Bothwell on my land, to goad me to madness, as his vile, lying tongue demonstrated. Reader, will you permit, in this year 1877, as treasonable conduct as can be found recorded in 1777? Southern slavery has been denounced; the battle fought, the victory won. The illiterate negro was permitted to vote who could not read or write; illiterate and unprincipled men were hustled into office until our land cries, as with the blood of Abel, for the souls crushed in this Northern Confederacy by malpractices of the statutes, of humanity and of decency. Reader, I appeal to you for assistance and protection against those malpractices of the law in North Brookfield and Worcester, where not a human look of chance for truth and statute laws against those moneyed men of my property are gathering sustenance to swamp me in financial ruin.

Oh, could you see that railroad board, riding in their stolen pomposity, taunting me with their employed tools (men). For instance, that North Brookfield bastard railroad runs so many trains per day, they stop on that four mile route as some of the pop-corn swells desire— take on baggage and let off the same, take on individuals and let off the same—as said railroad ring accommodations may demand. (The free rides come hereafter.) Coming up from Worcester one time, the train we were to meet at East Brookfield, an accident at Palmer despatch says, "start soon." We had waited more than an hour previous to the dispatch. I said to the man informing, "I will go to the store to pay a small bill; have I time?" &c. "Yes, they are at Palmer, you will have ample time." I went out, the distance I had to go was about twenty rods. The train immediately starts; the conductor, &c., seeing me leave the car; my store packages in car. I called for the train to stop, it being their practice for their ring. Nothing but laugh and hoot. Freman Walker roaring louder than the rest, as report has it. And such a jollification as that made in North Brookfield for a month pen cannot describe. That train due arrived in less than fifteen minutes after.

Another. After my imprisonment, I was coming up from Worcester—sick, just able to move—I dropped asleep in the car. The shout, "Change cars for North Brookfield," &c., roused me; it being the long express train, I was helped off by passengers at the freight-house. The conductor must have seen me, but he starts, as report has it, in two seconds and leaves me, the only passenger; and then another ha, ha! "Miss Hill left again"—a perfect pow wow. And Frank Drake has told, report says, I swore so and so. Reader, I said nothing, but asked to have my packages put into one, as I was very sick and might drop them, which was kindly bound together; two men urging the chances to carry me home for $1.00 and $1.50. I thanked them, and said "perhaps the foot exercise may be a recuperative, and the pleasant night is before me. Good evening, gentlemen." The stories that the railroad company sent out would fill a volume.

Reader, is there need of another Christ to redeem that Sodom of sin? You cannot fail to see those seditious beggars in power tramping a self-respecting and law-abiding woman with the most savage cruelty ever known in a civilized community. I ask you to do all in your power to aid me in vindicating the five different legal issues in this book, that the parties may be held to statute law and justice. As to my being a home-body. The citizens there, for the past few years, know nothing of my business, nor of my goings or comings. They are not my associates; I instruct them when employed.

The *North Brookfield News* has two attempts at suicide within twenty rods of the three churches during the month of October, 1877. And spiritualism has again established itself this said October, as in 1856, the time of the Waldo notoriety. There were at this era of Waldo, a Levi Damon and wife, and Calvin Hoyt and wife. Hoyt's wife enticed off Damon, and they live together as husband and wife. The forsaken Hoyt man and the forsaken Damon woman live together as husband and wife in North Brookfield's midst, in regular standing. A regular swap.

BIG SHOP NOTABLES.—Patrick Kellogg and wife were brother and sister,—now husband and wife; their father and mother being widower and widow. How does that compare with Fanny Fern's daughter and her father-in-law?

Monday evening, November 5th.—On the steamboat for New York. The cabin berths are all full except two top berths. I stay in the main saloon room. The wind is almost a gale. As soon as it is light enough to be out on deck I am there. The billow's foam sends forth spray with savage grandeur, and the cold, dismal looking waters are rolling up dense, black clouds, enveloping the sky in the rear with threatening aspect. Thus the last look on Massachusetts' horizon was tempestuous wind clouds, and as the waves headlong plunge and writhe in agony, a perfect hell of waters, tumbling like the sweep of destiny, rolling the clouds from its brink mountain high, leaving my native land in dark, deep oblivion. I walked to the side of the vessel, to the wheel cabin; the waves surge high, I bow my face down that the spray may wash it clean. It seemed as if it was God's opportunity thus to baptize me alone with the foam of the billow. And as I walked to the front of the deck, the pilot was pacing rapidly, as if to keep from freezing. My thought, my happiness on the water, I will not pen in this book—" Deep calleth unto deep." And what are we that hear the questions of that voice sublime? " Yes, what is all the riot man makes; bold babbler, what art thou?"

www.ingramcontent.com/pod-product-compliance
Lightning Source LLC
Chambersburg PA
CBHW020919230426
43666CB00008B/1504